Hidden Alchemy

*Remembering Your
Light Codes*

Jilliana Raymond

Hidden Alchemy: Remembering Your Light Codes

Copyright © 2025 Jilliana Raymond

All rights reserved. No part of this book may be reproduced in any form, in whole or in part (except for brief quotations embodied in articles, social media or reviews), without written permission from the author.

Published by

Softcover ISBN: 978-1-63618-126-4

Library of Congress Control Number: 2025927441

Book design by Deborah Perdue: Illumination Graphics
https//www.Illuminationgraphics.com
Call 541-862-7021 or email deborah@illuminationgraphics.com

Author photo by Claire Hageman

Some images in this book, including cover art, were generated using artificial intelligence (AI) tools provided by OpenAI's ChatGPT with DALL-E. © Jilliana Raymond, 2026. Some images were subsequently edited by the author.

Ellen M. Gregg
provided editing suggestions and spiritual support

Recognition

Creating any assembly of thought requires great effort. There are many individuals who provided support for this project and I'd like to acknowledge their stellar efforts.

A great thank you to my publisher, Aviva Press and the very capable hands of Susan Friedman.

No published work could be completed without providing the framework. To this I credit Deborah Perdue and Illumination Graphics for her superior design.

Behind this creation was the spiritual nudgings from very gifted channels:
Alysson Held Anderson and Ellen M. Gregg
My sincere gratitude for the spiritual feedback from Ellen and her team.

*The words within these pages are light infused.
Their role is to heal, empower and provide ascension codes
for all those ready to embody the vibration of light.
Take only the words that resonate within your heart,
allowing all others to unfold within the realm of
Divine timing or simply fall away.*

Contents

Meet Jilliana vii

In Her Own Words ix

Introduction 1

Origins 3
    Pleiadian Star System 8
    Arcturian Star System 10
    Sirian Star System 12
    Andromeda Star System 15
    Lyran Star System 18
    Venusian Star System. 20
    Alpha Centauri Star System 22
    The Moon 23

Soul Contracts 25
    Soul Assignments 27
    The Role of the Antagonist 29
    The Role You Chose to Play 31

Understanding Your Soul 35

Frequencies 41
    Earth Energy 43
    Sensing Energy 44
    Energy Vampires 46

    Events that Lower Your Vibration 46
    Thought Frequencies 48
    Healing Frequencies 50
    Light Frequencies 54
    Communication with Higher Frequency Dimensions. . . .55

Did You Know? 57

Creating Emotional Freedom 65
    Family Imprints 66
    Looking Behind the Scene 69
    Emotional Overlay. 70
    Timelines: Rewriting the Story 73
    Ancestral Soul Components 75
    Suicide 77

Living Consciously 81
    A Living Planet 81
    Environmental Frequencies 82
    What Can Be Revealed from the Healing Energy
    of Plants. 85
    The Consciousness of Storms 86
    Wisdom of Trees 88
    Experiment with Plants 88
    Animals and Their Healing Qualities 89
    Power of Words 90

The Alchemist Within 93
    Signs of Remembering Coherence 98

How to Receive Messages of Light 101

Remembering Your Light Codes 107
    Language of Symbols. 109
    Animal Messengers 111
    New Alignment with Intuitive Senses 112
    Calling in Ancient Allies 114

Life in Spirit 119
    Taking the Fear Out of Dying 120
    What Might My Spiritual Life Be Like? 123
    Preparing Before Your Last Breath 127
    Documentation of Assets 128
    Resolving Unfinished Issues 130

Anchoring Light Codes 131

Glossary 138

Recommended Reading 148

Author Resources 149

Testimonials 153

Meet Jilliana Raymond

Author, speaker, spiritual teacher, energy channel and healing master. Jilliana has been introducing individuals to the spiritual stewards who watch over us through her writing and teaching for over 30 years. In 1990, Jilliana began researching the energy components that contribute to individual life events in search of answers to her own life challenges. She has studied with life masters and world class healers in pursuit of the wisdom she shares with her audiences.

She holds an honorary doctorate in metaphysical healing. She is a continuing education reflexology instructor/practitioner who wrote her own healing protocol that addresses the residual emotional energy that becomes stored within the body's physical composition. Her healing toolbox contains therapeutic reflexology, craniosacral alignment, violet flame infusion, healing with the masters, as well as being a spiritual advisor.

Jilliana captivates her audiences as she explains the relationship between our physical and spiritual worlds. Her messages have been broadcast to millions through podcasts, speaking engagements, CBS, Voice of America, and through her writing. She is an international award-winning author distilling her discoveries into the powerful principles she presents to her audiences.

In Her Own Words

I find it interesting that some of the greatest spiritual channels, teachers, and energy healers began their spiritual exploration as extreme skeptics. Prior to embarking on their own spiritual adventures, these incredible leaders held positions as engineers, scientists, medical researchers, space explorers, educators, and life adventurers dissatisfied with traditional ideations. Many come from two schools of traditional thought: religious or agnostic beliefs. Most had no exposure to spiritual anything. In fact, most attendees at spiritual venues participated as reluctant "drag-alongs." Many were thrown into the realm of spirituality having no idea what that meant. Few, if any, had any previous awareness of some latent energy sensitivity, or intuitive ability, shuddered at the thought of multiple life experiences, or more than likely doubted any ability to connect to any spiritual force.

If anyone told me 35 years ago I would be writing, teaching, speaking or presenting spiritual anything I would have denied the idea insistently. I was a single mother raising two young sons. I was an exhausted business entrepreneur, family-oriented woman who was brought up with a traditional religious foundation.

I was literally thrown into researching anything that would help provide answers to the bizarre events I found myself experiencing. I have come to understand that the universe is an impeccably designed organization that can activate contractual agreements each of us agreed to before entry into this physical world. What I have discovered is that life alteration becomes the catalyst that promotes a new and better adventure for all to live a more rewarding life.

The timing of any life alteration is individual, but if embraced can be the most wondrous adventure of your lifetime. Several years ago I was considered to be a reluctant, curiously skeptical "drag-along." I needed proof of the unbelievable presentations during the many workshops I attended. And . . . I still need proof today of any emerging ideation, healing therapy or energy assessment. I'm a researcher. My focus is on healing . . . not only my life but those that I interact with. While not all of the new thought innovations would resonate with my specific energy frequency, the potential healing value any new innovation might provide to another is intriguing.

My encounter with anything spiritually oriented, other than my religious training, began following the death of my mother. It was a difficult time in my life. I was dealing both with her departure and the collapse of my 17-year marriage. I remember waking one night to visualize my mother's floating form entering my bedroom. At first I thought I was dreaming, but in my semi-altered space of waking reality; I rationalized myself to be a rather balanced, intelligent person. This experience would be the first introduction to spiritual encounters with many, many to follow.

My mother brought me the assurance that everything would be alright. There was no audible sound heard but a deep "knowing" this was the message she was delivering. She wore a mint green chiffon gown, her age appearing to be around that of 30. (I have since learned the age of 30 seems to be a popular presentation for those who have passed and returned to the physical realm to assure loved ones of their presence . . . and to give the bereaved reassurance that the deceased are thriving in the spiritual realms.) I am a rather logical person, so this presentation, although very real, seemed extraordinarily unexplainable to my newly activating spiritual awareness. I might add I came from a staunchly religious background. This experience caused me to question my belief system. Thus began my research into the unfamiliar "spiritual" side of things.

To help me process this, and many more phenomenal encounters, I enrolled in any class I could find that would provide any kind of answer to satisfy my natural curiosity. My religious training couldn't prepare me for anything so unbelievable or so enticing. I continue to pray that all could experience that one undefinable experience that would launch them into their own exploration. I was so excited about my discoveries I wanted everyone to see the magic within their own lives and to provide an undeniable connection to all things universally designed.

My second encounter with energy occurred after enrolling in a Reiki class. Reiki was a popular area of study at the time. I knew the instructor, so I decided to explore the modality. I followed the instructions carefully, musing over the excited outbursts from participants marveling as they felt the subtle energy field of Reiki energy. I felt nothing! I had a medical background so I was interested in anything that had to do with healing. I was determined to experience the sensation many others were exclaiming delight in. Encouraged to take the class a second time (and not one to give up) I enrolled again, and again I felt nothing! What's up with this? One could say I'm frightfully stubborn with a curious nature that begs resolution. After discussing the dilemma with my instructor I enrolled a third time. There is a saying, "third time's the charm." And so it was. I felt the energy ... what everyone else was so excited about. It was faint at first, and yet it was definitely detectable.

This encounter was over thirty years ago. I spent the next four years studying with the class instructor who, as I later discovered was an ascended master. Much of what I share with you was provided to me through my intense study with this master. And while his identity was never truly revealed, I have my suspicions into the depth of his mastery. I learned how to remote view, to visualize energy most are not attuned to see with their human eyes, to learn to trust in intuition, to look beyond the obvious and to embrace a healing energy that accompanies me to this day.

These early beginnings led me to the endeavors and discoveries I pursue today. I am considered an energy channel, an intuitive, a spiritual adviser, and an alternative therapy master. I tell this story to my audiences to demonstrate their inherent talents exist within them, even if they are unaware of their hidden abilities. I have been privileged to experience other dimensional realities that to most would be impossible, unbelievable, yet mesmerizing and awesome beyond belief.

There is nothing extraordinary about me other than my innate curiosity and tenacity not to give up. You possess the same ability to experience the spiritual dimension as I do. If all could embrace their spiritual identity there would be no reason to engage in conflict over religious identity, varying cultural diversity, land acquisition for exclusive power initiatives or political agendas designed to leverage authority over their constituents for personal gain.

No child is born with hatred in their heart. If humanity could remember they were born in love there would be no reason for disharmony. If all could remember their connection to an energy that is traditionally referred to as God/Yahweh/Source there would be no concern of lack or need for greed. All are children of God. All are particles of this great omnipresent source. You reside within the realm of all things magical and creative. There is no reason not to directly communicate with this energy who knows you better than you know yourself, who loves you despite what you may consider to be your flaws and is not a vengeful, retaliatory entity but a loving, forgiving essence of the Universe.

My discoveries are proof of life beyond any physical existence. I can only promise that if you are open to new concepts you will be wildly intrigued to begin your own cosmic exploration into your true identity. Once you begin your exploration you will learn how you can utilize energy to your advantage and become aware of a cosmic connection to spiritual resources that will assist you in optimizing your physical journey with love, understanding, and healing throughout your life.

Introduction

I'd like to take you on an alchemical soul journey to help you explore the depth of your ancient heritage. To understand life navigation, the first universal truth to comprehend is that the Earth matrix operates off two essential frequencies . . . Love and Light. All experiences . . . all challenges come from energy derivatives of these two frequencies; love representing the highest vibrational essence of your true makeup and light representing the energizing force that provides you with the momentum to experience life.

Tradition, ritual, societal constructs, and misconceptions often contribute to individual belief systems. What if everything you thought you knew about your living world didn't work quite like you were taught to believe? Many rely on historic texts to steer their lives. We could learn from historic anthologies but interpretations can be molded to present directives designed to provide steerage for a particular era. Anthologies are often written as historic representations or stories written as a way to interpret events experienced during a lifetime. The guidelines presented may provide wonderful ways to express life but can also be used as a manipulative tool to create a false alliance.

How else can we explore our living world? This book is in part a compilation of years of research, curiosity, and resolution to the profound opportunity that awaits the adventurer. Wouldn't you like to explore your soul and what makes it and you unique and special? What is certain is your lineage is ancient. The complexity of your soul is extensive. The extent of the universe in which you reside is infinite and life is eternal.

Are you ready to explore and discover your ancient legacy and awaken to your inherent light codes?

Origins

Archeologists, explorers and adventurers spend countless years exploring humanity's architectural, written and biblical history, just waiting to discover a clue about humanity's ancient history. Less research is spent on discovering ancient origins.

Long-ago clues were left behind, carved into the ruins of buildings, tombs, and ancient archeologic sites buried for centuries, giving us insight into our ancient roots. Translations of the depicted art and symbols became speculative as few could interpret the ancient languages, but their historic reference reveals volumes about our ancient roots.

If you ever watched a Star Wars movie then you can easily see how planetary explorations can take you to other star dimensions.

While you may believe the Earth is your predominant planet of origin, it is likely your soul's expertise has been gathered from multiple planetary systems over lifetimes.

Over the Earth's evolutionary journey it has been filled with dark history. More than ever, during the present chaotic field, there is greater importance for the "family of light" to be here now. If you are reading this material, then you are an integral part of this light force. You are part of a growing "Light" community of cosmic travelers to be the cosmic glue that unites worlds. There is a biblical reference that states *God sent his Only son to Earth to experience the physical suffering of Earth's inhabitants.(John 3:14) Jesus (Yeshua) came to teach humanity that all are sons and daughters of one Great Light.* Just like Jesus was the envoy for humanity so many years ago, God has sent many sons and daughters of Light to be here now to assist with Earth's ascension and to guide the Earth's inhabitants into higher dimensions within the galaxy. As Light Ambassadors, you are particles of the Great Is—God particles of one Great Light.

As Earth's humanity raises its awareness of their ancestral heritage, many planetary systems will evolve and raise their evolutionary frequencies as well. This is why so many planetary systems are invested in the Earth at this time and why they are assisting us during our physical journeys now. Their evolution is inherently entangled to the Earth's ascension.

Life is ancient and so is your ancestral background. Most individuals are aware of physical ancestral lineages, those reported affiliations with biologic relatives, but few consider their

Origins

soul's lineage. Your soul is comprised of much more ancestral exposure from varying encounters that did not originate from your familiar family ancestries. It's also comprised of experiences derived from life encounters designed by your soul throughout ancient lifetimes and just perhaps from off-world experiences.

Some information might seem beyond comprehension now, but just for fun take a moment to consider the plausibility of such information. If you are open to a concept that your origin might be from another advanced civilization in the universe you might find exploration through this writing, internet, and YouTube exploration to be wonderful resources.

I suppose I should define "Soul." Various dictionaries reveal a category of explanations to define an essence referred to as "soul." While the soul is thought and feeling, it is much more. It is the core essence of every living thing. Your soul is eternal. It is (you are) a multidimensional explorer having lived through centuries of experiences on ancient lands, holding memories from countless explorations, while fulfilling multiple life assignments. Your exploration is a higher expression of your perfection. Your soul is a record keeper for all your explorations expressed through countless presentations. It is a subconscious intelligence designing encounters that enhance the depth of wisdom you ironically chose to explore.

Although you are more than likely unaware of your ancient lineage, those entering the physical atmosphere of planet Earth have enrolled in a PhD course of study. No matter your star lineage, all entering the Earth's atmosphere are subject to pursuing areas of study based upon the individual's soul's design. And just to add some confusion into the matrix, most entering Earth's dimension do so under a temporary cloak of amnesia that enables the traveler the ability to master the chosen area of study without access to their prior experiences.

There are currently millions of galactic travelers on Earth referred to as "*star seeds.*" These galactic travelers come from many different constellations and galaxies around the Universe. They come with a specified mission to help raise the spiritual consciousness of humanity. They have a deep understanding of cosmic truth, universal laws, and understand humanity's greatest potential to achieve its highest frequency.

Origins

Thousands upon thousands of light masters came from the stars to merge among the human family to present messages of light. More than likely you've encountered at least one of these advanced souls as they walk among you. In fact, you may have galactic origins. Meet some of your galactic neighbors and see if any of their characteristic traits might align with your energy composition. Please understand these are artistic renderings.

Rendering from: Starseed584.artstation.com

Remember this guy? He's known the world over for his efforts to deliver messages of love and cohesion. His goal through his teachings was to empower his listeners to understand their Divine connections, but he had to overcome the fear, social, and cultural programming of the era. Religious and cultural programming molded individuals into their beliefs, which at the time prevented ascension for many. Humanity would largely fall into familiar patterns of living without realizing their compromising behavior.

While the life of Yeshua is seen as a physical embodiment, his dimensional home was, and is off world. Sirius is a star system of higher learning. It is the potential planet of origin for this ascended master.

See if any of the following galaxy descriptions resonate with you.

PLEIADIAN STAR SYSTEM

The Pleiades is a star cluster located in the constellation of Taurus. NASA indicates it's one of the nearest star clusters to Earth. Astronomers estimate it contains over 1,000 stars. Some may be familiar with the brightest of the star clusters referred to as the "Seven Sisters." It is thought this advanced civilization might represent many of our ancient parental origins.

Pleiadian Star Seed Characteristics:

Pleiadian star seeds are often healers and teachers, dedicated to spreading light, inner peace, and enlightenment. Those who resonate with Pleiadian energies often describe feeling different from others since childhood (a common trait amongst star seed individuals). They are typically described as "old souls" with uncanny depth, wisdom, and spiritual maturity beyond their years. A common trait is a driving sense of purpose to make a positive impact on the world.

See if you resonate with any of these characteristics that might describe a Pleiadian star seed.

- You are a powerful healer.
- You have a giving nature.
- You are kind and generous.
- You are empathic.
- Traditional medicine modalities can collide with your internal composition.
- You hate conflict and criticism.
- You are highly intuitive.
- You abhor cruelty and want peace to prevail.

ARCTURIAN STAR SYSTEM

Arcturus is a huge orange star reportedly 25 times the size of the Earth's sun. The planet can be seen just beyond the Big Dipper in the night sky. Arcturians are said to originate from a blue planet that orbits the star of Arcturus.

Arcturian Star Seed Characteristics:

➢ Arcturians possess astonishing intelligence and advanced psychic abilities.

➢ They are often visionaries and innovators, bringing new perspectives and solutions to the challenges faced by humanity.

➢ They are great orators and leaders.

➢ They can be viewed as arrogant or egotistical but this is not their nature.

- They are great mathematicians. They are well-versed in sacred geometry.
- They have telepathic abilities.
- They may feel like the "black sheep" of their family.
- They are not in tune with their emotions; therefore this is one of their lessons to master while on Earth.

SIRIAN STAR SYSTEM

Sirians are known as spiritual seekers. It is a planetary system of higher learning. These souls originate from a cluster of planets known as Sirius A, B, and C. These systems comprise the Canis Major ("Dog Star") constellation.

Sirians are said to have great influence with the ancient Egyptians, helping to inspire development of the Great Pyramids. Their influence is also evident throughout ancient empires of the world like the Dogon, Mayan, Olmec, Nubian, and Peruvian civilizations from ancient Ur in Iran/Iraq, and ancient advanced civilizations around the world.

Sirian Star Seed Characteristics:

Sirians are known for their advanced technological and spiritual knowledge. Their mission is to help advance human civilization through innovation and higher wisdom.

- They have a strong connection to water and are drawn to science.
- They have a deep love for animals and nature.
- They love researching lost civilizations, cultures, and myths.
- They have a natural curiosity to explore magic and mystical pursuits.
- They are even-keeled and very hard to anger.
- They have a few close friends instead of many casual friends.
- They have a love for arts, crafts, and writing.
- They have a relationship with one or more ascended masters.
- They can become bored easily. If they don't have something to do, you'll quickly find them fantasizing about new possibilities and solutions, and even creating new worlds in their mind.
- They can easily get caught up in the past if their Earth experiences have worn down their natural energy life force.
- They are devoted to their path or careers.

- They dislike social classification. Sirius is made up of lots of diverse and different energy types and beings. They can't understand why humans put labels on people and create segmental classifications within society.
- They like exploring spontaneous adventures.
- They prefer quality over quantity when it comes to personal relationships.
- They value trust, honesty, and respect over iconic pursuits.

Origins

ANDROMEDA STAR SYSTEM

The galaxy's name finds its routes in Greek mythology. The constellation was named after the mythical princess Andromeda, the daughter of Queen Cassiopeia and wife of the Greek hero Perseus. The Andromeda constellation is located in the northern sky, between Cassiopeia and the Great Square of Pegasus. It is the 19th largest constellation in the sky, occupying an area of 722 square degrees. The brightest star in Andromeda is Alpheratz. It is sometimes also known as Sirrah. The star is located 97 light years from Earth.

There is a hypothesis the Andromeda galaxy is spiritually linked to Earth's. It is also thought there are fewer Andromedans on Earth than other galactic travelers. Andromedans are the guardians of the seventh dimension.

Andromeda Star Seed Characteristics:

- Andromedans demonstrate a good balance between masculine and feminine energy.
- They excel in analytical thinking and creative pursuits.
- They inspire those around them to explore their own energies, encouraging them to break free from societal norms and embrace their true selves.
- Many of them feel out of place since they cannot understand how humans can be so closed-minded, inconsiderate towards other living beings, and brutal because of some personal issues, which most likely came from childhood trauma.
- The majority are light-workers who chose to walk through life choosing love over fear. They are optimists keeping hope alive even though they have had their fair share of challenging experiences.
- Their auras reveal luminescence.
- They are quiet and tend to stay in the background as observers.

- ➢ They have a strong desire to travel.
- ➢ They can be emotionally guarded and avoid conflict as much as possible.
- ➢ They may be tall, thin and some may bald easily.

LYRAN STAR SYSTEM

There are few stars in the Lyra constellation, but the main planet of origin is Vega. One proposal on galaxy origination is that the first humans originated from Lyra. Two races of ancient beings called Felines and Avians (does anyone remember Avatar?) also come from Lyra. Lyrans helped establish much of the ancient world on Earth including Atlantis and ancient Egypt. Lyrans are typically found in the higher dimensions.

Rendering from Mx.pinterest.com – Reubin - Lyran Healer

Lyran Starseed Characteristics:

➢ Lyrans are good with animals.

➢ They have a strong connection with cats.

➢ They have the ability to shift consciousness easily.

➢ They have an intense curiosity to research lost civilizations.

- They often have dreams of drowning. This may have an association with Atlantis.
- There is a magical fascination with the Sphinx.
- They are musically talented.
- They are artistic by nature.
- They enjoy social environments but prefer to be the observer.
- They are fiercely independent.
- They generally present a positive, uplifting personality.
- They see things from a higher perspective and see the most minute details clearly.

VENUSIAN STAR SYSTEM

Venusian star seeds live in the fourth dimension. They are called the Hathors. Hathor was an ancient Egyptian cow-goddess representative of love and motherhood. Venusians are here on Earth to teach love and compassion.

Venusian Star Seeds:

While this beautiful soul looks as if her Earth home could be any tropical environment, her peacefulness demonstrates how star seed individuals carry a galactic vibration that is representative of an off-world origin.

- Venusian star seeds are often tall and slender.
- They are sensual and passionate individuals.
- They are highly spiritual beings.
- They are very connected to the universe, their higher self (soul), and guides.

- They are hugely in tune with their metaphysical compositions.
- They are drawn to ancient Egypt, and more specifically they relate to the goddesses Hathor, Venus and Aphrodite.
- They are interested in alternative healing modalities.

Hidden Alchemy

ALPHA CENTAURI STAR SYSTEM

Alpha Centaurians come from the Alpha Centauri star system. Alpha Centauri, like its galactic cousin the Pleiades, is the closest star systems to Earth. Science has confirmed there is a habitable planet within the Alpha Centauri star system. Alpha Centauries are an advanced civilization whose purpose is to assist Earth in her spiritual expansion.

Alpha Centaurian Starseed Type:

➢ Your favorite color is purple/violet.

➢ You most desire a career in the scientific field.

➢ You possess a high intelligence.

➢ You enjoy research in biology and chemistry.

➢ Attainment of knowledge and wisdom are a top priority.

➢ You enjoy quiet space and are often uncomfortable in crowds.

➢ You are independent and confident.

THE MOON

The depiction is a representation of Thoth in ancient Egypt. In Egyptian mythology Thoth was revered as the god of wisdom, writing, and the moon. He was depicted as a man with the head of an ibis and was thought to possess magical and intellectual knowledge. He is considered the patron deity of scribes and scholars.

As the god of writing, he was seen as the protector of scribes, who were responsible for recording information, maintaining administrative records, and preserving religious and historical texts. In addition to his association with writing and wisdom, Thoth was believed to govern the lunar cycles and was associated with the concept of timekeeping. *Havefunwithhistory.com*

Movie and TV fantasy adventures have presented us with an array of characters from Star Trek, and Star Wars, Lord of the Rings and Avatar. These renderings may not be far off from a host of galaxy star seeds. Galactic Earth travelers may not present in their off-world embodiment but prefer to blend with the appearance of their human cousins. However, they may retain several tell-tale differences. Their energy bodies may glow with radiance. Their eyes may be captivating, often blue, radiating light. They may have a calming energy field and individuals may be drawn to their magnetism.

Their Earth embodiment usually presents with at least two missions. All come to refine some soul characteristic, as well as to implement some teaching element to the human family. Some may come to deliver new technology and all are masters.

When you accept the potential of galactic individuals walking amongst humanity, your new awareness signifies you carry more light. When you carry more light, those you encounter benefit from the light infusion you leave behind. When your soul radiates love, and others begin to incorporate more love, this causes a planetary regenesis. When you work with the Light, you can unlock your own Akash (your personal soul record) and remember more of who you are and the importance of your Earth mission.

Soul Contracts

*E*veryone is on an evolutionary soul journey. Your presence here on Earth is not by accident. You answered a clarion call that was sent throughout the universe long ago . . . asking for the greatest souls in the universe to be on the planet now to assist with the elevation of consciousness.

Unbeknownst to you . . . long before you came to Earth to explore your life journey, . . . you had a hand in designing your life. That means you chose most of your life experiences . . . even the ones you weren't aware would be so challenging.

For those who have encountered a life challenge, the first question I might intercept is, . . ."Why would I create something so challenging?" I remember asking myself this same question when faced with my own challenges. I voiced my response to Spirit acknowledging, "That was really dumb!" . . . vowing to make better future choices.

Every individual currently living on Earth has a life purpose, a soul lesson to master, a past life to heal, an ancestral life to either embrace or release, a life role designed to provide some life catalyst for personal change and ultimate higher frequency resonance, a life role to help another to heal, a life purpose to teach another an important life lesson, or to become part of the Earth's light family of ascension.

As you prepare for your Earth life, you begin to explore an array of options. You choose the curriculum best designed for your goals, you select the lessons you desire to master, you determine how many hours of study you think you can maintain (you did enter the PhD program of universal life study), and you choose the study environment in which you will enact your life expression. You choose the parents who will raise you, the location of your incarnation (country and state), the language and customs of your society, and those you will encounter throughout your life journey. You had a hand in arranging it all.

You might choose one of those less desirable life programs that might include poverty, homelessness, illness, addiction, disability, or any individual acting as a catalyst for change. Make no mistake . . . these assignments represent the soul choices of a master.

While you may think you are a separate entity and not part of a grand consciousness, you belong to a group study collective. What you learn and share with your group and the Universe may prevent another soul from having to undergo a similar challenge. Your collective will learn from your experience, thus everyone will benefit from your program.

SOUL ASSIGNMENTS

There are a myriad of life experiences to explore that will expand the knowledge you are seeking towards your degree in Earth Magic. Throughout your evolutionary journey there are required areas of study. You might compare this to those non-elective choices that come with any degree. In other words, there are some life inclusions that are non-negotiable. Either there is something you need to resolve from a previous life encounter or there are required experiences to master in your particular chosen area of study. You might even have to revisit a life journey with a former adversary you'd rather not engage with. This is where the term "karma" comes in.

I prefer the term "accountability" because in essence we are all responsible for the favorable and unfavorable interactions we share with individuals. Most notable to understand here is there is never any blame, shame, guilt, or judgment placed upon the soul traveler from any universal source. You, the Earth traveler, place the burden of guilt upon yourself and then spend lifetimes trying to erase and repair the emotional residue you inflicted on another and upon yourself. This is one of those non-negotiable areas of study you must master and provide resolution to. This is why Earth school is so difficult.

Each time you encounter an experience less desirable, you can implement change to alter the direction and the outcome by redirecting your focus. This does take a little concentration on your part and some creative redirection. Forgiveness is the best way to start. This isn't always easy, especially if during the life journey the emotional intrusion was exceptionally harsh. Understanding forgiveness can offer a different direction in thinking. Consider the energetic components you carry when you are unable to forgive an individual who you feel has compromised your life. The energetic weight you carry around with you is the equivalent of dragging a ball and chain behind you. It is part of the entanglement of energy constantly reconnecting back to the offensive opponent. I'm not one to lend any of my energy to an opponent whose personal directives differ from my own. Forgiving is not necessarily associated with forgetting. You may not forget the intrusion but you disassociate your energy from the person and event.

When faced with any uncomplimentary life challenge it takes tremendous inner reflection to switch the negative banter into a positive outcome. During these encounters it is unlikely you remember you are wearing a spiritual cloak. What you think could be a life mishap might just be a life opportunity. In actuality, the encounter was a well-rehearsed dramatic segment designed while in your spiritual house that would present at some designated point (that more than likely you are not aware of) during your incarnation. This catalyst might be the dramatic infusion that presents you with a new direction of opportunity.

Once you have chosen your study program, you bring your selections to your guidance team. They review your choices and try to steer you away from those lessons they believe might be too challenging. You then begin to finalize your curriculum . . . Simple . . . right? . . . Not so simple. It seems the harder the life curriculum is chosen, the more advanced the master soul.

While housed within a spiritual environment, possibilities are endless. Study programs are generally pursued without conflict. There are no adversaries in spirit to deter you from your path or discourage you with regard to your desired achievement. And ... while well-meaning guides attempt to prevent you from adding too many challenging study programs to your curriculum, you are undeterred from achieving those soul goals you have aligned for yourself. One important note here: While you might be able to accomplish soul expansion in your spiritual house, your evolution can take much longer to accomplish than designing the same program while evolving in a physical dimension where duality exists (light versus dark). This is another reason why any individual would attempt to absorb as many life experiences as possible. And, as any of us who have traveled through physical life expressions knows, the best teachers are those who have direct experience with a particular program.

Many years ago, I attended a speakers' conference where I met a couple whose subject matter was divorce and the single parent. I inquired of the couple if either of them had any direct experience in such matters. Both replied no. How can you be an expert about something you have no experience with? The phrase "walk a mile in my shoes" comes to mind here.

THE ROLE OF THE ANTAGONIST

No child is ever born with an emotional overlay of hatred or fear. It is a learned behavior. If the child is brought up in a loving environment, the child will most likely retain its loving foundation. Observation of injustices, exposure to individuals behaving badly, being raised in a house with conflict, growing up in war-torn atmospheres . . . these are the ingredients that become the causal factors of limitation, fear, and hatred.

As in any movie or TV drama there are often antagonists that present an opposing character, the villain everyone wants to dislike. And way too often in our current environment we are experiencing many individuals who are over-playing their antagonistic roles. Let's be clear about one thing: Annihilation of a group of souls for the sake of greed or power is not an acceptable role.

In a matrix of duality, the role of the antagonist is a contractual assignment. And not to make this principle too confusing, not all antagonists are created equal. While some souls choose to play the antagonist as part of their soul contract, others become the antagonist purely through their ego's choices. For example, Hitler's abhorrent actions (including annihilation of a group of souls) were the result of his ego, not a soul contract. I'm sure you can apply the actions of current antagonists whose activities are not part of a soul contract but an egotistical drama.

At an appropriate initiation to comply with the original design of a soul contract, an unconscious program activates and an opposing character role emerges. This was a special assignment requested from a higher source and confirmed with your acknowledgement to become interspersed amongst all your chosen assignments that you agreed to before your descent onto

Earth. Let's also be clear: The role of the antagonist is almost always enacted through the character portrayal of a master soul. You and your antagonist enter Earth school to play out the drama, forgetting your spiritual natures. Remember, this was an agreed upon role designed to enhance some aspect of your soul's design and to propel the human family onto a more optimal way of living.

Just as an actor often forgets their lines in a play, once in Earth's atmosphere, exposed to challenging life circumstances, it is easy for the antagonist to forget their role and attainment of the desired outcome. The plot becomes twisted when either party involved in the drama goes off script. An emotional overlay develops and the original script has taken on a new, perhaps more sinister, composition.

THE ROLE YOU CHOSE TO PLAY

Your parental choice provides you with the foundation for your Earth exploration, giving you a genetic head start on the specific lesson that will enhance your soul's evolution. If your life endeavor is to pursue a specific life achievement, you may have chosen parents who already have a foundation in the pursuits of your choosing. If your life goal is to teach, perhaps your parents were educators. Perhaps your family alignment will provide you with a financial head start to help you accomplish a pre-determined business adventure. If your life goal is to design a specific invention, provide a cure for disease, or accelerate a designated field of research, your DNA may have been infused with the DNA of your parents to assist in accomplishing your life goals. Say you want to play a specific sport and your parent is a recognized athlete. Your parents might pass on genetic characteristics to provide you with features that would support your career goals.

Some thirty years ago I embarked upon an explorative journey into a more complete awareness of my physical and spiritual composition. The catalyst that initiated this exploration was a desire to understand why I attracted difficult life challenges. Perhaps like you now, my initial research was not always in alignment with my fundamental life understanding. I grew up within a religious framework with life circumstances exposed to the traditional protocols of cultural and societal expectations of the current time. Those earlier beliefs did not seem to align with the research I was pursuing but the discoveries were irrefutable. Because of the challenges I was exposed to and the research I was investing in, I was aligning more with greater understanding, more spiritually connected, with a greater wisdom within my own evolving world.

Through the courage to overcome a challenge, you are teaching resilience to another. No one can truly know what choices any of us will make when faced with an assortment of life challenges. You could theorize how you may react when faced with any life alteration, but unless you have direct experience with a presenting challenge you may not be able to adequately access the knowledge or support required to provide a solution for another. It would be wiser to reserve criticism regarding another's life unless you're fully comprehending the complications of that individual's unique challenge. Those who have direct experience with difficult life scenarios become the best advisors to help guide those who are or will experience a similar incident.

Understanding Your Soul

Your soul is on an evolutionary journey. Its goal is to provide you with as many experiences as possible that will add to your personal book of knowledge. In addition to the study program you chose to pursue, your soul included its own agenda. Each additional program is designed to refine a missing element in the soul's composition.

You present valuable information that you are continuously sending into the galactic ethers to report on the conditions of life on Earth, all while learning how to master specific lessons you and your soul designed specifically for you. You provide the wisdom gleaned through every challenge you have ever faced to a universe filled with souls wanting to learn through your experiences. You are the living masters on this world now. You have made many sacrifices to be here. All eyes from a grand universal audience gaze upon your accomplishments and your hardships with awe. Your watchful guardians acknowledge that the journey is not always easy but the benefits are enormous.

There have been times in my life when I did not think I could take one more step. In fact, every great master that has entered a physical world has endured many challenges. Every one of them experienced great doubt. They may have momentarily lost their faith, no matter how spiritually oriented they may have been. And they may have called for assistance from a higher source on multiple occasions only to have been reminded that they were never alone and often supported with Divine intervention.

Perhaps by now you are aware there is much more than one life to live. No young souls are reading this material. In fact, most of you are such old souls you have been part of an ascension team for millennia. It is possible, however, that a past life experience might be contributing to your current life assignment. Everything you surround yourself with reminds you of some aspect of a past life. Look around your residence. What artwork signals your heritage? Where would your travels take you? In fact, if you have the privilege to travel to distant lands, you may be walking in previous footsteps from a past-life destination. If any life fragment from your past travels remains within that environment and you travel to that land on one of your explorations, you will most likely feel some reincorporation of any lost soul fragment. I have found over the many years of my research that any time I can discover another piece of my composition it provides a better comprehension of who I am.

Perhaps like you now, my initial research was not always in alignment with my fundamental life understanding. While training has provided much of the knowledge I embody in this life, it is my supposition that past-life incorporations have aided in my current life pursuits.

I am also quite certain that your collective lives have contributed to your own life scenarios. Your roles will have included wondrous journeys, as well as those you would rather forget. You have been masters for many of your lives but all in all you have accumulated wisdom throughout your various encounters to become the individual representation of who you are today.

It's almost as if there is an internal clock keeping time on the events in your life. Think of this internal synchronicity as the activation of a subconscious program that goes on line at a precise moment on your physical journey.

Soul lessons are infinite. One of the more difficult incorporations is to learn to love you. This can become a difficult assignment when faced with overwhelming criticism and judgment. This is a man-made overlay and not a soul initiative. You are a perfect design just as you are but you are relearning how magnificent you truly are. The body suit you wear is not reflective of your magnificent light, or of your intergalactic appearance.

The soul wants to you to learn to overcome fear. This is another man-made construct . . . and I might admit it can be restrictive and extremely difficult to ignore when faced with so much chaos in our current world. We must employ more faith that there is a divine plan in place and that we are constantly surrounded with loving assistance from the spiritual dimension, even if we don't ask for it.

While on the topic of faith, your soul wants you to employ more of it. And again, when faced with a barrage of unsuspected challenges this can be daunting. When immersed in the navigation of life challenges it is easy to forget we are surrounded by a flurry of angelic and spiritual support.

Soul lessons can include overcoming addiction, becoming self-reliant, overcoming feeling abandoned, learning that you are "good enough," not needing to prove to anyone of your personal reflection, setting boundaries on acceptable behavioral issues, accepting cultural and individual diversity, learning to let go of issues out of your control, and not interfering with another's soul lesson. If you are aware of a perceived characteristic deficiency, this more than likely is a soul lesson needing to be mastered.

As a parent mastering learning to let go is a difficult lesson. I had a saying when my sons were expressing youthful exuberance that I needed to let them play in the street while hoping they wouldn't get hurt. Of course this was metaphoric and totally unrealistic.

I also suppose this lesson follows closely with learning to trust. This is another huge lesson for me. In a world fraught with illusion, it is often hard to separate false presentation with reality. It is easier to let a universal guidance system that always sees 360 degrees become the steerage system in life. I liken this reference to that little voice that comes from within that warns of impending drama.

In some past life your role may have taken on the scenario of King Midas. During this exploration all your desires were met. You now find yourself learning to be self-reliant and wondering where your abundant security will come from. Here's where trust comes in. Too many are faced with financial uncertainty or survival issues as familiar lifestyles suddenly become totally rearranged. While you may have mastered one lesson, you now find yourself mastering the opposing scenario.

Another lesson is learning patience. I know several individuals struggling with this lesson, especially given congested cities, extended traffic delays, long wait times for this or that, or limited resources. I'm sure you can add your own pet peeves here.

And . . . I've saved the best for last . . . Forgiveness. I don't know anyone who hasn't had an issue with this scenario. It is the hardest to accomplish and the most rewarding with regard to freeing us from entanglement. Just saying you forgive someone, without truly internalizing the emotion, creates no long-term benefit. I can send forth a blanket forgiveness statement and surround the world in it. But when I attempt to fine tune the emotion within my own composition I need to truly be sincere before the desired benefit can be achieved.

If you find yourself reviewing the same familiar scenarios that present with a new twist, it is your soul's reminder to you that a little more effort needs to be applied to the compromising lesson.

Frequencies

Society teaches us to seek religion to find answers. No one was taught to seek frequencies. Everything has an electromagnetic field and everything functions through vibrational fields created by an electromagnetic impulse. I'm going to refer to these fields as frequencies. The frequencies are represented by band-widths stimulated by sun-lit infusions (the solar system). Everything upon Earth is vibrating at different frequencies ... These variances include the products you purchase, the food you consume, the people you encounter, and the places you visit. Energy is the air we breathe, the water we drink, and the sun that nourishes us. Every country, city, and neighborhood carries its own frequency. Most Earth inhabitants may not be aware that the land and environment in which they reside carry their own energy frequency. Each frequency is generated by the collective inhabitants of that region.

Whether you are consciously aware of your personal energy field or not, every individual has a unique energy signature just like a finger-print. Your individual signature is constantly assessing the energy matrix it is exposed to. All souls enter the Earth's environment with a high-vibrational core energy. None start out intending to be the latest terrorist or narcissistic dictator du jour. Certainly no one desires to become the latest offender or victim. None need endure life-threatening disease because of a toxic frequency that individuals may have been exposed to. You should now understand that all are influenced by whatever energy exposure defines their life experience. All are shaped by those individuals that filter in and through their lives. All are influenced by family relationships, cultural traditions, those we define as teachers, leaders, lovers, and friends. All contribute to the fabric of your energy matrix.

While you navigate through your daily activities you are constantly threading through energy pathways. Wherever your travels take you, you are absorbing and transmuting the various energy frequencies that you encounter. Perhaps your travels have exposed you to individuals who have unknowingly absorbed toxic elements from their exposure. These individuals are highly empathic and highly sensitive to the energy frequencies they are in contact with and largely unaware of their toxic interference. If all your encounters represent positive influences, then your physical experience will more than likely be insulated from any toxic exposure. Your positive reflection then will attract opportunity and synchronistic encounters that mirror your optimistic mindset.

If, on the other hand, you are surrounded in an environment that reflects a negative atmosphere, these encounters will contribute to a toxic lifestyle. If you perpetuate recycling life patterns that are unhealthy to your well-being, these unpleasant patterns and their toxic effects will become amplified in your experience.

So what does all this mean? If there is any portion of your life that needs balance you will need to adjust the incompatible energy exposure. This will affect relationships, jobs, health, where you reside, anything you experience in your daily routines. Understanding your personal energy contribution provides an accurate review of how well you navigate your current world, thus allowing change to occur when you identify any toxic exposure.

EARTH ENERGY

Currently, the Earth's energy frequency is changing. This energy adjustment is necessary for several reasons. Earth energies are long overdue for a major transformation. This could explain the volatility Earth inhabitants are currently experiencing. What Earth inhabitants are noticing is a new balancing of energies.

Most will agree, full moon energy has a tendency to invoke some odd behavior. Some individuals are more sensitive to the energy magnification the lunar events create, but it's not just lunar activity that creates an energy fluctuation. Consider how many varying geomagnetic events affect individuals. Geomagnetic events include accelerated solar activity, astrologic planetary repositioning, or internal Earth events such as volcanic activity and continental planetary shifts.

Sensitivity to the Earth's magnetic variances can leave one feeling lethargic or energized, agitated or just aware of an energy difference. If you are a pet owner you may be aware that your fur baby seems to be reacting differently to some invisible force. And just as you may react to the enhanced energy frequencies, the Earth reacts to the emotional projections of her inhabitants. This can create more volatility in storms or anomalous Earth activity. I'll discuss this further in the chapter *Living Consciously*.

SENSING ENERGY

Did you ever wonder why you may be attracted to a certain region over another? Or why you shop at a favorite store and avoid another? If you plan on attending a seated event did you know automatically where you will sit or why you choose to sit next to one individual over another? Your subconscious energy field has been assessing the energy field long before you arrived.

As an example of energy assessment, say you are looking for a new residence. You have searched online and now it's time to drive by your location. Pay attention to your surrounding area. You don't want to live next to a landfill, an electric grid that might interfere with your frequency, a flood zone, a dry zone (unless you enjoy the desert), a volcanic zone, or what I'm going to categorize as a "dead zone" (living in close proximity to a cemetery). You definitely don't want to reside near any battle zone that could compromise your energy or present you with any number of long-past residents popping in for a visit.

Frequencies

You want to reside next to pleasant neighbors surrounded by a pleasing environment. But how are you going to accomplish this? You're going to sense the energy in the area. Ask questions to see how you internally respond to your inquiries. How well-kept is the neighborhood? Do neighbors wave as you pass by or do they look suspiciously at you? If you sense a pit in your stomach (a little flip flop of anxiety) or if what you were hoping to see does not meet all your expectations, this is not a compatible energy for your specific field of sensitivity.

In contrast, if you get excited about the location, and you feel exuberant about the potential property, your subconscious energy is acknowledging your enthusiasm and potential compatibility. If you purchased a home from a prior owner, your home may carry the residual energy of that owner. In fact, if your residence has historic value you may have acquired the residual energy of its long-past inhabitants.

How will you tell? Do you get the willies when you walk inside? Does hair stand up on your arms? Do you feel like your hair is being played with? I live in an historic town where many local restaurants and homes have auxiliary residents. Most of the residual inhabitants are friendly, but if you reside near an area that experienced violent conflict, it is best to look elsewhere for your perfect residence.

I am used to living with a ghost and have even felt protected by one when I lived on a battlefield. But this may not be acceptable for you. For millennia, long before our current residence upon ancient lands, colonization has often been at the expense of indigenous peoples where there is most likely an abundance of lingering souls.

If you are interested in moving into a new housing development, you may want to research the prior land use before signing a contract.

ENERGY VAMPIRES

You encounter power struggles when you are exposed to individuals whose own energy is weak, thus necessitating an energy infusion from a higher vibrational source. Regardless of your ability to visualize energy fields, your subconscious field is always aware of surrounding energy frequencies. The lower vibrational field is always seeking a higher vibrational energy source to infuse its reduced energy status. It is always easy to determine when you have become the source of an energy picnic. Your energy body begins to recognize the negative drain as sudden fatigue, onset of nausea, headache, uncharacteristic irritation, or emotional lability. Empathic individuals are exceptionally susceptible to unknowingly absorbing lower frequency energy fields, especially if they have not insulated their energy fields sufficiently before stepping out into the exterior world of frequency.

EVENTS THAT LOWER YOUR VIBRATION

Energy systems can become unbalanced through any number of natural intrusions. This can be initiated through strong emotions of grief, trauma, illness, or social disruption. At the core of energy drains is fear. There seems to be plenty of that mucking up the world these days. In addition to the complicated human element is an assortment of relationship incompatibility. Added to this complex could be any sudden life disruption through any number of Earth or weather anomalies. In an instant lives can be disrupted presenting anyone with a new layer of coping.

Broadcasting networks love a good story. Usually the storylines are meant to keep us on the edge of our seats. It could be the latest terroristic fray, looming weather event, political mayhem or dysfunctional "Can you believe that." Most news broadcasting is designed to distract you from events behind the scenes. Did you know that repetitive sensational broadcasting can be toxic to your health? The repetitive nature of news can become so distressing that the accumulating negative energy can actually cause toxic overload.

This energy settles in your emotional body. I'm not suggesting that we ignore daily current events, but I am suggesting that we react less to the sensationalistic side effects of the latest news alert and learn to filter reason into our current assessment.

If you are involved in a negative confrontation, it is always best to first remove yourself from the source if possible. It is often a case of you being in the wrong place at the wrong time where you become the closest energy to receive the uncontained emotional expression. Simply recognizing the toxic exchange as a power drain can provide you with the wisdom to handle the situation. Elevating your energy frequency can be as simple as visually surrounding the individual in a bubble of white light, asking silently for angelic infusion, and understanding their sudden outburst more than likely has nothing to do with you. Instead, it's an emotional overlay they don't have the understanding to process or eliminate.

THOUGHT FREQUENCIES

Every thought is a frequency. Every frequency is a doorway. As a conscious traveler you begin to notice which thoughts don't belong to you. All thought creates future activities in our lives. You are a co-creative energy, so understandably thoughts become the vehicle that creates the events you experience. Thoughts are not powerless concepts. Thoughts, coupled with intense emotional fueling, result in rapid manifestation. Keep in mind that the intention behind the desired result can work for or against you.

I'm passionate about teaching and demonstrating how the power of thought and energy in our language directly impacts the life you experience. I can think of no better way to demonstrate the power of language than to present you with the results of an experiment conducted by Dr. Masaru Emoto, a Japanese educator and scientist. Dr. Emoto wrote several books on his experimental discoveries with water. One of his books,— *Hidden Messages in Water*, documents Dr. Emoto's experiments conducted on jars of water in a classroom environment.

To begin his experiments Dr. Emoto exposed various written expressions affixed to jars of water. One set of beakers received toxic expressions. Another set were exposed to loving expressions. Dr. Emoto instructed his students to express audible language to

Frequencies

the beakers. In addition, Dr. Emoto exposed one set of beakers to loud abrasive sounds and the other to soothing melodic sounds. At the conclusion of a twenty-one-day period Dr. Emoto photographed frozen sections of the water from each of the experimental containers. Water from beakers receiving positive projections produced purified water crystals. Water taken from the containers receiving negative frequencies produced distorted, incompletely formed crystals, the quality of which mimicked the appearance of cancer cells.

Purified water crystal

Pictures of Dr. Emoto's resultant experiments are depicted within his work *Hidden Messages in Water*.

If spoken or written words can have this impact on water, imagine how words impact the events in our lives and on one another? Add the power of emotion, amplified by the intensity of a delivered word, and the power unleashed can inspire or destroy any projected target.

What can be learned from Dr. Emoto's experiments? What happens when our thoughts/words are applied to the human body? If an expression of love can change the shape of a water crystal (and consider the human body is approximately 70% water), what effect do you think thought and word frequencies might have on human cells? Or for that matter, what effect do you think sound and accompanying intonation directed at a specific object might create? If sound can alter the composition of a water crystal, imagine how sound could also change the composition of a cellular structure.

Scattered thought distorts a vibrational field. Focused thought bends reality. Thoughts are sacred instruments not random noise.

HEALING FREQUENCIES

Sound Energy: Sound vibration is just one in a group of new emerging therapies. Music has played a huge part throughout history in gathering people together. There is a concept that the universe was created through sound vibration. If there is any factual truth to this statement, then it stands to reason why we

Frequencies

are so drawn to sound and its varying vibrations. In fact, NASA reports that the moon is a big bell and, theoretically, if struck with a hammer the moon would present sound.

If you'd like to conduct your own sound experiment, start with two plants, play soothing sounds to one and rap to another. Do this for approximately one week. See how each responds. The hopeful result will show that the plant exposed to melodic sound will appear to thrive, while the plant exposed to the harsh tones of rap may look lack-luster.

The exhilaration we feel when exposed to music can explain why we are so drawn to music. While all should be familiar with the benefit of relaxing sound, more investigation into sound frequencies and the beneficial harmonics of Hertz frequencies are being explored.

There are many websites that allow you to explore sound frequencies. Frequencygenerator.com and Hertzharmony.com seem to present simple formats for your research. In addition, you might want to research the healing frequency compilations of David Sereda and Royal Rife. These frequencies, along with their indicated benefit, can easily be found on YouTube. Each gentleman catalogued frequencies that would align with a particular dysfunctional element an individual might be experiencing. There are hundreds of frequencies to choose from. The theory is that by listening to the sound frequency the body would begin to harmonize with the sound field and balance the dysfunctional element.

Individuals may not resonate with all the Hertz frequencies.

Should you find it difficult to listen to a particular Hertz frequency, it is an indication your particular system is not in harmony with that particular vibration. There is a theory that every individual is missing one frequency that, when discovered, will align and balance their entire physical system.

Here are samples of Hertz frequencies and their accompanying potential benefit for the listener.

40Hz

Flickering lights and sounds at 40 Hertz have been used in Alzheimer's therapy to stimulate increased neural response and fight symptoms of dementia. Sound at 40 Hertz has been linked to gamma brain waves and the stimulation of memory.

174Hz

This is a Solfeggio frequency, a series of tones used in sacred music that is believed in alternative medicine to have different positive effects on human health. 174 Hertz is associated with the reduction of both pain and stress.

285Hz

285 Hertz is also one of the Solfeggio frequencies and is supposed to activate cellular regeneration, encouraging the body to heal itself in the event of an injury.

324Hz

This is a frequency that works with generating muscle tone.

396Hz

This sound frequency is associated with the removal of fear and other negative feelings. 396 Hertz frequencies balance the root chakra while simultaneously transforming negative emotions into positive, joyful ones.

417Hz

Healing sound therapy involving 417 Hertz also focuses on balancing negative energy, especially when trauma is present and helps to dissolve emotional blockages.

432Hz

432 Hertz therapy is targeted towards the heart chakra balancing, as well as prompting higher levels of mental and emotional clarity.

440Hz

Music that is tuned to 440 Hertz aids in cognitive development. Sound frequencies at 440 Hertz are considered to activate the third eye chakra.

528Hz

528 Hertz is one of the most well-known and popular of the Solfeggio frequencies. This musical tone is known as the 'miracle note.'

639Hz

639 Hertz is a sound frequency that affects the heart chakra.

This sound frequency is associated with greater attunement to harmonious interpersonal relationships.

852Hz

852 Hertz sound frequency helps with mental clarity, supporting an individual to redirect intrusive thought patterns. These thoughts may be associated with depression and anxiety. Exposure to this sound frequency can help alleviate the role of negative thoughts in these psychological ailments.

963Hz

The term "God frequency" is often associated with 963 Hertz. It is generally thought 963 Hertz sound frequencies are associated with activation of the pineal gland and higher spiritual development.

These are just samples of Hertz frequencies. And as I alluded to previously, the work of David Sereda and Dr. Royal Rife with sound frequencies may be highly beneficial when used in healing applications.

LIGHT FREQUENCIES

There are many descriptions on how light is measured. I selected this definition as I felt it to be the simplest. According to Stouchlighting.com, "Light is measured in lux, lumens, and candelas units. Lux measures illumination, indicating how much light falls on a surface, while lumens measure the total amount of visible light emitted by a source, and candelas measures luminous intensity in a specific direction."

The sun's energy is measured in lumens. The lumens are converted to watts. The intensity of the lumen (or watt) is determined by any number of astrologic ingredients including solar flares, magnetic resonance, and the weather.

Life on Earth requires the sun's nourishment to provide stability for food resources, cellular regeneration, and a host of beneficial associations. It is said that one bright candle can light up an entire dark room. As you represent "God Light" your presence can illuminate the world around you, just by your presence. Doesn't this all make sense?

Currently medicine is incorporating more light-infused therapy including refined laser procedures to remove diseased tissue. This causes minimal invasion to surrounding tissue allowing for faster healing and thus preserving energy resources.

Light frequencies are being used to reprogram neural pathways. Radiant light also presents healing benefits for individuals with bone or joint issues. This can be infused through any variety of light therapies, including amethyst light healing and red light therapy. Quantum light frequencies are also being used to reduce inflammation in tissue and provide overall cellular support.

COMMUNICATING WITH HIGHER FREQUENCY DIMENSIONS

Spiritual guardians reside in higher vibratory dimensions. These guardians are not some ghostly remnant of a white cloudlike appearance but an individual entity that has "walked in your shoes," and knows you far better than you know yourself. They have traveled lifetimes with you and have had previous experience in a physical dimension experiencing the very scenario you chose to experience. It took lifetimes in a physical world for these guardians to absorb experiences so they could be the mentor you need to help guide you in your current experience.

When you become emotionally compromised through an assortment of life intrusions your energy becomes dense, blocking communication with the very spiritual energies that can provide the comfort and the reassurance you may be seeking.

Spirit understands human fragility and will make every effort to reach out to help soothe fractured moments in a manner that will resonate with you without causing you to be frightened. Learning to breathe deeply and to remember to ground to Earth energy should provide you with the balance you need to regain your higher vibrational field and re-establish connection with the higher dimensions.

Did You Know?

Here are some interesting concepts to ponder. Allow the information to settle before discarding the insight. I remember searching through a library of titles many years ago wondering what some book titles were referring to. My brief exploration of content at that time was beyond my comprehension. Energy builds in frequency until the vibration in matter matches the content of the wisdom seeker. Looking back today with more understanding and research into the materials, I'm able to see the value of those titles that made no sense earlier. Today, I continue to search for materials that will expand the wisdom I continue seeking and capture my adventurous curiosity to discover more about life and its navigation.

I want to provide a fundamental spiritual understanding of a great energy all refer to with many different identifications. The energy referred to as "God" may have had a physical presence at some point in galactic history. However, no galactic alliance seems to remember any time frame or reference to such. Throughout millennial civilizations, however, there have been documented some 970 names that cultures have used to describe a great conscious awareness.

Many years ago, I pondered one of those curious titles that didn't resonate with my understanding at the time, but caught my eye. The title was *All That Is* by James Slater. What could this title possibly mean? With many years of research and an internal working comprehension of most matters spiritual, I now have the answer. The divine vibration of an omnipresent Source is "All That Is." You cannot be separate from a Divine source because you reside within its omnipresent vibration. God, Source, Yahweh . . . regardless how you reach out to this Divine presence isn't essential. What is important to know is that God is all things.

Life on Earth today (largely due to astrological positioning) is ending a millennial cycle and entering a new era: the Aquarian Age. This is perhaps why everything in today's world seems so volatile. As one cycle ends everything changes. You've possibly heard of the "great shift." While everything seems presently chaotic, anything that is no longer compatible to your intended harmonic design is being illuminated. Anything that no longer serves your human vibration, your fellow life traveler's vibration, or the Earth's vibration can remain. All are presently feeling the epicenter of the shifting vibrations as the Earth enters her millennial metamorphosis.

There has been much discussion on the creation of a new Earth. In fact, this is becoming a reality. It isn't that two different planets are being created, allocated as Earth I and Earth II. It's that variable frequencies will determine which energy matrix you will reside within. If your belief system relegates you to a structure of limitation, anger, chaos, control, etc., you will reside on the complimentary Earth plane that will continue to support your belief system. If, however, your belief systems are open to new thought, to living in a more harmonious way, to becoming more receptive to newer concepts of learning, then you will reside within the prism of that harmonious Earth network. Your vibrational frequency will determine which environment you will reside within. The concept of a new Earth was never about a new planet revealing itself but about a difference in belief systems and vibratory fields that denote the environmental equivalent of its residents.

For those desiring to accept a different matrix to live within, humanity is moving into a new dimension, one without social or cultural contamination. Within the new playing field there are no limitations. Compassion and harmony are the ingredients of engagement. Thought in motion becomes the mechanism that will create the desired life events.

Consciousness can only expand as far as individual belief systems will allow. Too often individuals have been influenced by childhood observation that has created a limiting view of their environment. If a child is not allowed to freely express their internal awareness but instead instructed how they need to feel and react, their belief systems may become molded by society or cultural programming. Only when a major interruption prompts change will the belief system be re-examined, and then likely change. Belief systems that become anchored into a person's reality become crystalized. Once crystalized the ideation becomes more difficult to change the perceived thought on what is reality. This is why constant exposure to a toxic environment, social restriction, constant programming meant to control and manipulate must be overcome.

What is out of balance must return to balance. Everything you do in this life matters. You are literally creating how you experience your life by how you react to the events and challenges you face on a daily basis. If you project fear, negativity, hatred, anger, that is the reflection you will create. The ideation becomes a magnet to draw to you what you focus on most. If your mirror is that of positive focus, you will attract love, opportunity, emotional freedom and harmonious life experiences. Everything you do in this life becomes the navigational highway for your experiences.

Centuries ago some very wise viziers developed ritualistic systems through which they could project authority and establish guidelines for the people of that era. As each vizier's reign ended and another took its place a new set of concepts arose. These ancient ritualistic practices became the early versions of religion. Religion became the pathway for individuals to communicate with a higher source. Only when individuals learned they could directly communicate with God would the ritual no longer be necessary.

Today religion serves much the same purpose but adds a layer of social community to its resume. Ritual still remains, along with years of anchored belief systems, making it hard to introduce any new thought on the subject matter. This isn't to say that religious houses don't contribute a wealth of beneficial services to a community, all done within a loving atmosphere, but religion isn't or shouldn't be a one day a week practice. Religion's cousin, spirituality, should be a living expression.

I can't imagine too many are unfamiliar with the artistic representation of a golden halo surrounding the head of the Virgin Mary and the baby Jesus. The halo was meant to be a representation of their spiritual mastery. Ascended masters (if we are able to visualize their auric fields, the energy body that surrounds all living things) have attained that same enlightened aura. The aura isn't an affirmation of Christianity (a belief system many ascribe to as followers of Jesus); the aura is a spiritual energy signature that is represented through the frequency of light. The Christ energy notation is considered to be the essence of universal recognition for any who have attained spiritual enlightenment, not the identification of an iconic avatar.

More Fun Facts

When God said "Let there be light," God sang the Earth into being with the "Om" vibration. Sound created the Universe. Frequency transmutes everything into light.

Dead Sea Scrolls were written on parchment . . . Parchment was not available in the Middle East during the timeframe of the life of Jesus. Essenes were the scribes of the Dead Sea Scrolls but these were written after the life of Jesus.

- What if what is referred to as spiritual (not to be confused with religion) was encoded technology? Just a thought.

- The Universe responds not to what you want but what you believe. Your focus will determine what manifests in your life. If you believe in fear, you will attract it. If you believe in loss you will find ways to fulfill it.

- Inner criticism is planted. Someone somewhere has repeatedly shown you how to be critical. Inner doubt is inherited. Someone somewhere taught you not to believe in an inner confidence that you could accomplish anything. Shame is absorbed. It is a learned behavior you inherited and then repeated.

- You are not the name you were given. You are not the story you inherited. You are a master soul having a physical experience.

- Most people don't create their lives; they live in a programmed loop of navigation disguised as logic. Focus on how you wish to experience your life, not on how you are experiencing it.

- Stone circles are alliance matrices. Pyramids are megalithic transmitters.

- Giza pyramids are a giant clock.

- Meditation with symbols is the architecture of original

thought. Spirit best interprets communication through visualization.

- Temples of Atlantis had no books on shelves, only rooms of vibration.

- Did you know the reason for the blessing of the meal ... and for that matter any time someone sends you a blessing ... is to change the molecular structure to harmonize with the vibration of the sender?

- Artificial Intelligence, when used appropriately, was given to humanity to raise the planet's frequency.

Did you know the body maintains energy centers known as chakras? Chakra is a Sanskrit word from India meaning "wheel." Each chakra center governs a different segment of the body's energy system where nerve centers within the governing system merge.

The first three chakras are associated with one's personality. These chakra systems generally include the root (the first chakra), the sacral (creative center) or second chakra, the third chakra representing the solar plexus or identity center.

The second harmonic centers are linked to the fourth, fifth and sixth chakras. These centers can be referred to as the soul matrix. The fourth chakra is associated with the heart, the fifth chakra correlates to the throat and the ability to express oneself completely. The sixth chakra represents the third eye or the center of intuition.

The seventh, eighth and ninth chakras are associated with the crown chakra and represent contact to our over-soul matrix.

The archetypal fields of the tenth, eleventh and twelfth dimensions represent the fourth Harmonic Universe. This dimension is the home of many Master vibrations.

The thirteenth, fourteenth and fifteenth dimensions represent the energy dimension of star councils, the angelic realms and where Master souls reside.

Humanity is now in the Age of Aquarius or the age of the chalice bearer. This refers to being keepers of the Gra*al (Templar depiction of the true translation of Grail). This was the symbolism of the Last Supper . . . that humanity held the sacredness of life. The "Holy Grail" as referred to in many religious houses, is considered the Grail, or chalice bearer. The Gra*al are the keepers of Light.

Creating Emotional Freedom

Most of your life has been shaped by default, echoes from parental fears, social distortion, a lack of personal understanding of your archetype, astrologic influences and how you respond to all these factors, but much of the distortion you respond to is not represented in truth. Stress in the family line can create separation from your sovereign source, especially when love has been challenged. Separation from Source can lead to unresolved generational patterns in the future if left unresolved. Through acknowledgment, understanding, and forgiveness, it is possible to heal any family or personal crisis from the past. Any release or healing of traumatic memories with love and understanding ripples out to all time in that it positively affects and reinforces all generations and lineages throughout time.

Throughout your life you are constantly storing memory. Your subconscious is recording the emotional impact of all the events in your life. Favorable events create momentum along your life journey. Unfavorable events, either observed or experienced, become obstacles that need to be overcome. While your conscious programming may attempt to override the emotional memory, until you address the root imprint and rewrite the memory, it will continue to resurface. (See discussion under *Timelines*).

All emotional entanglements can impart residual influences that carryover into your current life history. Life experiences can become teaching elements for the soul. If a chosen lesson is ignored, the lesson repeats, each lesson presenting with greater intensity until it has been fully realized. Many challenges can be imposed when hidden vows, curses, or karmic issues from a previous life are unresolved. These character inclusions became part of your embodiment during that century's practices because of the suspicions misunderstandings of the time.

Once the restrictive vow is recognized, you can ask for removal of the declaration and healing intervention from spiritual guardians. Accompany this with a personal invocation releasing you from the previous vows recited during a past life and you will resolve the life restriction imposed on the soul by you from a previous declaration. Your invocation might be formatted this way..."*Release me from any vow, curse or restrictive invocation that no longer compliments this life journey.*" When said with authority, the restrictive element will quickly dissolve.

FAMILY IMPRINTS

Somewhere during your formative years someone may have presented you with an idea you wouldn't be able to accomplish

Creating Emotional Freedom

a goal because of some life restriction. This may have left you with a mental imprint that could prevent you from achieving a lifetime dream. These verbal or activated imprints may have sidelined the spiritual course outline you designed before your entry into the Earth dimension.

How often can you relate to disappointment or make a connection to an emotional flare initiated through any combination of relationship interactions? I can't imagine too many escape some recall that continues to sabotage progress throughout a life. Surely parental influence becomes the foundational system that establishes your emotional fabric. What you learn and inherit from family imprints usually sets the foundation for your creative life experience. If you are taught to love and grow within a supportive and benevolent environment, you will hopefully maintain that positive influence. If, however, your life observation is one of turmoil, restriction, and condemnation, it becomes more difficult to separate from the foundation you have become accustomed to during your formative years. This foundation now becomes the subconscious memory that, if not changed, can sabotage future life navigation.

When you are young you have no access to insights that would allow you to block the intrusions. But as you become aware of the sabotaging effect absorbed from often well-meaning individuals presenting you with their own interpretations, with acquired wisdom, you will now be able to distance yourself from any acquired limitation.

To help you understand compromising behavior, Carolyn Myss wrote a wonderful interpretation on individual archetypes in her book *Sacred Contracts*. The archetypal field represents patterns in an individual's emotional composition with explanations why you may have chosen the archetype to overcome the missing lesson from your soul's composition. You could be learning to overcome abandonment, to become self-reliant, to love all aspects of you despite your presumed unfavorable self-assessment. You may have chosen an archetype that would address a self-limiting behavior making you feel you're not good enough, or somewhere you absorbed an imprint that wouldn't allow your voice or input to be heard. Then there is the list of "don'ts." These intended protective imprints also define limitations within the personal psyche.

Life surrounding the family structure can explain familial customs and life expressions that become passed down through lifetime lineages. Too often parental imprints can be transposed upon their children. These imprints come from the misguided parental lineage and not from that of the child's inner knowing. Now, as an adult, you're still trying to release the false imprint you absorbed from your parent(s). These imprints come from their unresolved emotional imprints. Perhaps your parent is still coping with unresolved abandonment, unfair abuse from a strict parent, alcoholic or drug intoxication that would keep the parent from remembering the emotional impact of their youth, or worse still, the lack of love or acceptance from their parental rearing.

Life is complicated, so to help understand the present behavior, look at the parental past life equation. My parents

Creating Emotional Freedom

went through a depression, a world at war, social inequality, monetary scarcity, rationed resources, and abandonment. Women's place in society had limitations preventing them from being heard or having any social platform. If they married well their life might be secured. If they were single they had limited choices. What common thread of life can you correlate between your relationship with your parents or siblings at this time?

Too often families carry the guilt or shame from past family events. What if your role in this life is to release and clear those past life traumas? The undertaking of this challenge can be as simple as invoking intervention from spiritual guardians or from past ancestors (if known). Solicitation should ask for release from the associated trauma or from a current scenario connected to an evolved lineage. You can acknowledge the incident but also help the residual soul to comprehend the misunderstanding by removing any emotional charge or psychic wound associated with that life drama.

LOOKING BEHIND THE SCENES

Sometimes conflict arises when engaging in differing relationship opinions. I have always found it helpful to look behind the scenes to determine why conflict has arisen. If you are close to this individual you may know what their childhood was like. This could present some clue associated with their emotional compromise. Is a family member sick? Is there concern over budget matters? Are you experiencing the backlash from their previous encounter? Conflict is rarely about you but a prior encounter, an unresolved memory, an insecure feeling, and much too often a fear. The message here is that it always pays to examine what is causing the imbalance that created an incident before you become entangled in conflict.

EMOTIONAL OVERLAY

Something you consider to be an undesirable characteristic within you may in fact be an emotional overlay inherited from another. You could have inherited the imprint from a parental authority, a revered caretaker, or friend. This inherited imprint could also be a genetic marker. Not all genetic markers are indications of an inherited anomaly. Unless you scripted this detail into your soul contract you may not have inherited the imprint from a biologic source. I could have addressed this under family imprints, because that is what this is . . . but you will need to determine if this is a characteristic that belongs to you or something imposed upon you from another.

All false belief systems that create an emotional impact can live in your physical body until the excess emotion becomes so toxic it emerges as disease. Disease is the result of those accumulated life frustrations you were unable to completely process at a specific time because of a lack of understanding of the causal factors. Those belief system imprints have now become the structure of your living dimension. I used to present a workshop titled "What's Toxic in Your Life." It might be helpful to write down those issues you feel are contributing factors to your present toxic interference.

Start by being vigilant in eliminating propaganda constantly streaming to us through an assortment of media that loops the listener in a constant embellishment of fear. The programming tries to keep you on the edge of your seat to distract you from living a more fulfilling life. I'm not suggesting becoming an ostrich paying no attention to current events but I am suggesting you become less enraptured by the content.

The body is a wonderful storage system. It remembers everything . . . from the smallest insult to the more significant one. While in youthful body armor subtle imbalances are less noticeable. But with age the toxic overload surfaces. As an alternative therapist I have a strong desire to help individuals live life to its maximum. I am trained in reflexology. I knew reflexology was an incredible way to reduce stress to relieve accumulating tensions. To compliment my knowledge of reflexology, I enrolled in a program that would identify underlying emotional causes that could become housed in varying organs. The emotional underlayment became the mainframe of dysfunctional ailments. The foot became the perfect tool to identify the emotional residual. Some 5,000 years ago in China the art of reflexology was developed mapping the entire physical structure of the human body within the framework of the feet. The skilled hands of the practitioner could identify the organ systems and massage the area to provide release. The foot then became the catalogue to assess the emotional fabric of its owner.

At the time of my studies, there wasn't an alternative modality that would address the emotional impact within a relaxing framework, so I wrote my own massage protocol to address emotional imprints held within physical structures that I could identify by massaging the feet. I call the therapy Integrated Sole Energy Therapy.

As a practicing reflexologist, my intuitive and sensory field can detect where this information is stored. If my client is open to receive the information that will release an emotional cause, with focused energy I am often able to open the congested corridors allowing free flowing energy to prevail. My clients receive and experience a renewed energy field.

Following is a list of organs where emotional overloads occur and the reason behind the energy congestion:
- Adrenal Glands – Being on edge
- Bladder – Shyness/Helplessness
- Circulatory System –Being guarded as well as the body's gatekeeper
- Gallbladder – Unresolved resentment
- Heart – Loneliness, Lack of joy, lack of self-love
- Kidney – Fear, Broken will, shame
- Large Intestine – Unable to let go
- Liver – Rage, Anger
- Lungs – Grief, chronic sadness
- Small Intestine - Insecurity
- Spleen – Low self-esteem
- Stomach – Anxiety

TIMELINES: REWRITING THE STORY

In a physical Earth template there is what humans consider to be a timeline; a linear measurement to denote a day, month, or year. In a universal template there are a multitude of parallel realities playing out simultaneously. Visualizing time as a continual loop of events and time expression seems to lose its value. This can be correlated to changing a channel to present different programming.

If the Earth traveler can visualize an uncomplimentary event and wishes to rewrite the story, this can be accomplished by recalling the unfortunate memory, then beginning to rewrite the story. The idea is to replace the memory with a favorable memory you'd rather recall. Over time the old memory will no longer be able to be recalled. The new memory will only be that of a pleasing content. When you can no longer recall the memory you will know that the event no longer can create an emotional restriction that you have been carrying for lifetimes. This will unlock all parallel timelines now and in the future.

Here is an interesting concept. I presented you with the paradigm that most disease has an underlying emotional foundation. And once an individual can identify the underlying emotion the presenting symptoms would resolve. Trauma is often accumulative. It can begin in childhood, become buried in the subconscious until some trigger awakens the memory and dysfunctional symptoms start to appear. Louise Hay wrote *You Can Heal Your Life,* a wonderful book that summarized presenting ailments with the emotional cause, that once identified, would allow the individual to reflect upon the resolution to release the emotional impact that was presenting in the body.

I don't suspect many of us have escaped some compromising scenario in our lifetimes, but understanding where an insult began helps to direct resolution. This doesn't mean you erase the event. You simply release the resonance that's fueling the programming. You're not really changing the story, but you're changing the signal that causes you to react to the memory.

To completely eliminate emotional attachments to a past trauma, resolution may need to be introduced during this life to prevent continuation into future generations. Changing past emotional conflicts allows you to alter those vibrational patterns that lower your ability to enjoy life more. Once you have released the memory and thus the emotional attachment, your current life activities will be filled with opportunity and adventure. Your new optimism and freedom will also transfer into future lives. By resolving past emotional traumas, you forever change the lives of your sons and daughters through the success of clearing the ancestral lineage. This is referred to as entanglement.

Consider this exercise to help you clear unwanted life patterns. Visualize life as a film reel and each frame is a different event representative of your life. Go as far back as your film reel will allow you to recall. Find the frame on your picture reel that presented an emotional impact in your life. If there have been several you will need to address each separately. Become the observer of the situation, . . . even if it is displeasing to watch.

Visualize as many details as possible. You may want to write your findings down so your paper memory can be discarded at a later point. You may be able to hear audible reflections as you recall the events. You are totally surrounded in love from your spiritual team as you proceed through the exercise so there is nothing to fear. Your highest outcome is all your spiritual team is concerned about. If there are multiple frames accompanying a traumatic foundation, take one frame at a time, replacing the unfolding drama with more pleasing interactions. Do this as many times as necessary until you feel you have successfully rewritten the programming that is causing your current symptoms. When you are successful at creating a new memory pattern, you have rewritten your life programming.

ANCESTRAL SOUL COMPONENTS

Most individuals are aware of physical ancestral lineages but few consider their soul's lineage. Your soul is comprised of much more ancestral exposure from varying encounters that did not originate from your familiar family ancestry. It's also comprised of experiences derived from life encounters designed by your soul. In addition to family ancestral components you carry the residual memory of your previous soul life and too often the unresolved emotional impact from an unanticipated life challenge. Your soul life may engage several ancestral families and not be limited to your current physical family.

Your soul is a multidimensional explorer having lived through centuries of experiences on ancient lands, holding memories from countless explorations. Research into past soul lives will explain much about personal traits and reactions to repetitive events that may present as compromising events during this life.

Some souls linger in an etheric dimension caught in an endless loop of bad memory. These "lost" souls generally remain close to the environment associated with their traumatic ending. Some of these "trapped" souls are unaware that they are disconnected from a physical body, and most are unaware that all they need to do is summon spiritual intervention (This would be a spiritual guardian, angel, or ancestor) to assist them in crossing through the dimensional veil.

Most of us are familiar with the endeavors of paranormal researchers. Many investigators attempt to scientifically validate the essence of some presence lingering in homes, abandoned buildings, historic landmarks, and areas where violence, death, and extreme trauma have occurred. No matter what is discovered through the scientific lens, many logical or rational attempts to solve such metaphysical occurrences can never completely provide the answers why the spiritual essence of a trapped soul remains. The soul is either unable to return to its spiritual dimension or has chosen to linger in an etheric realm to resolve some energy conflict . . . all while awaiting for a doorway or portal to open for the trapped soul to return home.

If you notice recurring themes and patterns that continue to replay throughout your life, this could be an indicator of a certain blueprint in your ancestral lineage.

SUICIDE

I want to address the topic of suicide to help those who have experienced this trauma in their family engagements. Many religions disavow a soul that has ended their life prematurely. Too often this stigma shrouds a family with the shame and guilt associated with the cumulative events that may have led to the individual's inability to cope with presenting life issues.

More than likely the soul carrying this ancestral scenario is attempting to clear something from a "soul family" perspective. From a spiritual perspective this has *NO* bearing on the record of the soul, nor from the perspective of the parental family, or from the viewpoint of any associated individual emotionally attached to the individual. There is no guilt or retribution invoked upon the soul who has chosen to end their life prematurely. This is a social stigma.

In my family's history there have been four suicides in this lifetime. This unfortunate history provides me with many significant details I need to be aware of. I carry the unpleasant family legacy of premature death through suicide. This is much like those who have inherited a gene from their parental DNA. I must be mindful of the predisposition so when faced with emotionally compromising situations I must dig deeply into my own psychic composition to overcome the emotional thought of a premature departure. Secondly, I need to honor the lives of those who found the only solution to their internal suffering was to find a way to end their mental anguish through suicide.

As a spiritual council I can appeal to the higher consciousness of the individuals who have found the only resolution to their mental anguish is through suicide, acknowledging the difficulties each encountered, providing them with a deeper understanding of the life lesson they chose to overcome. I can remind each that they are divinely loved and ask each what is necessary from their mental perspective to help them release the trauma they have endured. Too often the emotional impact was an inherited overlay from a close individual. Once a new perspective can be applied, this provides whatever bolstering for their spirit is necessary for the individual to continue their life journey and release the scenario from occurring in the future. Reminding an individual embroiled with the emotion of failure that their life mission was to overcome the emotional negativity absorbed in this life is usually all that is necessary to release the compounding trauma.

If a soul prematurely exits before mastering a soul lesson, they will return to the physical dimension, bolstered by countless years of star-lit guidance and with greater determination to overcome whatever challenges that may present. This renewed spiritual infusion should suffice to allow the life traveler to complete the journey. Once again to be clear, there is no condemnation from a spiritual perspective for any soul that has prematurely departed. While that soul may need to re-enter a physical domain to overcome the life scenario and revisit the lesson where it began, there is no shame or failure label associated with the initial traumatizing event.

One final note on the subject ... while sorrow may linger for grieving family members wondering how they could have helped their loved one or why the troubled individual took their life, their beloved family member is renewing their spirit surrounded in the loving arms of the spiritual domain.

Living Consciously

A LIVING PLANET

Indigenous peoples have long known about the intricate balance of nature. Ancient indigenous cultures lived off the grid honoring the resources the land would provide. They studied the land, observed how their resources interacted with the seasons. They harvested what was needed for sustenance preserving the abundance for future needs.

Consider the possibility of the Earth being a conscious energy as the Earth responds to the conscious energy fields of her inhabitants. Webster's Dictionary defines consciousness as: " . . . awareness, being mentally awake or alert, done with awareness or purpose." In addition to a definition of consciousness, Webster's provides a definition for "soul." "Soul" is defined as "an immaterial essence of individual life . . . a spiritual force, that which has essence or consciousness." And just to add a little more thought into the equation Webster's defines life as:

" . . . the quality that distinguishes a vital functional being from a dead body or inanimate matter." If these definitions can be applied to the planet and the environment in which you reside, would this awareness change your perception of your living world?

Living consciously means being aware of your human footprint and personal impact that is imprinted with everything you do. Gaia is the conscious mother of the planet. From Universal watchers, Earth is referred to as the emerald planet. It is considered a planet of higher learning, a planet of great diversity and a planet of incredible beauty. Earth travelers upon this emerald gem are intended to be the custodians of the abundant resources provided for our sustenance. It is plausible the human impact upon the Earth can deplete resources intended for survival and pleasure. When we learn to conserve all resources, respect all living things, the Earth will rebalance and renew once over harvested sectors. Nature's design is far more impeccable in her awareness of the intricate balance between all species than her industrious human inhabitants.

ENVIRONMENTAL FREQUENCIES

The planetary energy grid affects every country, individual city, or neighborhood of residence. Each area carries its own frequency. The frequency of each country, city, environment, or residential area is generated by the collective energetic frequency of the inhabitants of the particular region. In other words, the Earth responds to the emotional energy of its inhabitants, collectively and via specific location. Becoming sensitive to the collective energy of the land allows you to determine where your particular energy field will be most compatible.

Of late, the Earth has also been dealing with astrologic pulses from the sun and varying planetary alignments. The study of astrology takes years to perfect but can become enlightening when explored to understand how the different planetary trajectories effect how we individually navigate through life. This planetary positioning also effects how the Earth responds to magnetic stimulation. Just as there is a cyclical rhythm in nature, there is also a cyclical rhythm within the planets. When planets are reversing their trajectory it is referred to as retrograde. This can cause edginess amongst planetary inhabitants. When the planets are progressing forward (referred to as direct) and the planetary configurations are in alignment with your birth cycles, this allows smooth navigation through your daily activities without the resistance of a reverse planetary flow. I bring this to your attention because how planetary alignments connect geomagnetically, directly impacts how you react to the energetic pulses you ultimately become exposed to.

Recently the planetary rotations within the Earth's cosmic network have presented Earth inhabitants powerful magnetic infusions. This is occurring through solar flare activity, rare planetary alignments, and an increase in lunar and solar eclipse activities. Every magnetic impulse is causing realignment within every living thing on the planet, as everything is absorbing the energetic infusions from the planetary alignments, sun activities and solar and lunar events. The projecting frequencies (referred to as downloads), are shifting conscious fields to provide coherence and renewal. This can be reflective in the increased weather anomalies, volcanic and earthquake activities. Although alignments of frequencies can at times seem heavy and sluggish as we attempt to make sense of the energy registration within our bodies, these magnetic pulses are releasing energy from shifting planetary plates preventing more destructive forces from occurring.

Do you remember the movie *Medicine Man* starring Sean Connery and Lorraine Bracco? The movie was released in 1992. Sean Connery played a doctor exploring the Amazon for a cancer cure derived from a rare flower. This flowering plant required a certain tree to grow upon that was found only within one region of the Amazon forest.

In the plot, a group of enthusiastic land developers were clear-cutting the very portion of the forest housing the specific trees and the flowers growing upon them. In actuality, the story line had roots with the Shipibo Tribe shamans (indigenous peoples living in the Amazon basin of Peru). These shamans carry ancestral knowledge of healing plant medicines. Today Shipibo shamans invite a select group of individuals to study with them to learn how incorporating the frequency of plant medicine can provide healing elements to individuals. Incorporating the healing elements of plants can vastly raise one's vibrational essence, providing insulation from invading viral introductions.

WHAT CAN BE REVEALED FROM THE HEALING ENERGY OF PLANTS?

Indigenous tribes have known for centuries about plant medicine. This knowledge was passed down through ancestral lineages. Somehow it made it to "Grandma's kitchen" to become the healing remedies from the past. Apothecaries started emerging in the sixteen hundreds, but not until the 19th century did the use of pharmaceuticals become widespread. Today modern chemists make their fortunes devising one remedy after another, all with noted side effects, that are often toxic to the user. All chemical formulas however, have their root foundation in plants. Before pharmaceutical companies began controlling the remedy market, Herbalists were researching their own therapeutic remedies. With the rising costs of pharmaceutical based formulas to address a multitude of discomforts, renewed research in to the benefit of herbal supplements as preventative solutions has regained popularity.

Herbal remedies can be found in natural teas. Lion's Mane mushroom powder can improve cognition. Dandelion root can reduce skin inflammation and improve the digestive biome, the Babachi plant can trigger collagen repair, and Sambuca can provide immunology support at the first sign of a cold, with so many more natural remedies that can be applied.

Conservationists provide vigilance over depleting resources. With education and awareness inhabitants can learn to be cognizant of all interactions with nature. None of us can afford to turn away from the destruction of resources. We may not understand the intricate reliance of one species to another, but the loss of one species should be cause for concern. We may not always have the awareness behind the need for a specific organism or species, but Gaia is the designer of these kingdoms and must have greater intelligence than our own to determine the interactivity and purpose for each. As guests upon this conscious environment, humanity definitely needs to be mindful of how each is living within Gaia's realm.

Our very lives depend upon our living consciously, reducing our personal imprints, learning to recycle; to be conscious of how we interact with our environment so that it will support us for millennia to come.

THE CONSCIOUSNESS OF STORMS

Did you know that Gaia mirrors the emotional fabric of her inhabitants? With continued emotional volatility Gaia has been expressing her voice loudly. For years I have been watching storms, their paths, the severity, and the type of weather events globally. I have pondered the conscious trajectory of each, the magnitude of energy, and the purpose of their steerage.

Storms act as clearing vortices. While storms inevitably cause destruction, often displacing inhabitants, and rearranging lives, in its path there is ultimate clearing. Winds clean the air and usher in renewal. Storms can restructure landscapes. They can warn inhabitants of a need for relocation. How is it that the animal kingdom seems to have advanced warning systems of an impending storm that prompts them to vacate an area before its

Living Consciously

landing? This is an intuitive sensory mechanism that alerts them to impending danger.

Years ago the HeartMath Institute began researching the impact of emotion on humanity. The institute conducted years of research in conjunction with the Hubble Satellite. Their research documented emotional signals registered in space derived from the collective consciousness of the Earth's inhabitants, especially during exceptionally volatile or celebratory events. How could Hubble register an emotional signal in space if consciousness didn't exist in space? If the Earth is a conscious planet that responds to the energies upon her, then doesn't it stand to reason that Earth events (volcanic activity, earthquakes, floods, fires, tornadoes, hurricanes, and the like) might respond to a conscious frequency of its inhabitants? My opinion is a resounding "Yes."

If storms have consciousness then it is likely the storm trajectory could be attracted to the presenting frequencies present in that region? Do you think your Light consciousness could reverse the trajectory and reverse the damaging elements of a storm? And again, my answer is a resounding "Yes."

When individuals become aware of their magical powers it is important to understand the potential necessity for a storms trajectory, before engaging in the reversal of steerage. This is where consultation with intuitive guidance, asking if engaging in efforts to redirect an imposing threat, is in the highest interest of all. Consideration needs to be entertained taking into account what new impact could present with a new storm direction. If you can develop communication with a specific storm or Gaia, it is possible to ask for the purpose of the storm and if engaging in reversing a trajectory is possible. At the very least it is possible to appeal to the consciousness of the storm or Earth event to diminish its impact.

WISDOM OF TREES

We all know how protective any mom can be protecting her babies. Had you thought this might apply to the consciousness of trees? According to a Smithsonian article, (March of 2018) a "wise old mother tree will feed her saplings with liquid sugar, warn neighbors when danger approaches and begin to launch protective measures." Wow! According to Peter Wohlleben (a German botanist), trees are connected to one another sharing water, nutrients, and sunlight. Furthermore, trees detect scent, experience pain when cut and send out electrical signals similar to the wounding of human tissue. Trees can sense danger and launch a chemical attack to discourage an intruder while warning surrounding trees of a pending onslaught.

According to some extraordinary emerging experiments, trees can count, learn, and remember. What vast knowledge could a tree provide absorbing the experiences of its inhabitants over centuries? It would be a wonderful experiment deciphering the messages.

EXPERIMENTING WITH PLANTS

We all know that plants provide medicinal properties. Plants provide shelter and the resources to build lodging and provide the oxygen necessary for life on our planet. Plants remove toxic particles in the air returning the environment with clean air. Crops provide an abundance of nourishment, as well as an array of showering flowers. Would you believe that plants emit sound? Experiments are currently underway to explore the healing frequencies of plants that can shatter cancer. (Remember the movie "Medicine Man")

Yale University School of Environment has been conducting experiments on the topic of plant sound. Using a device called the "midi-sprout" students are able to extract sound from plants. They discovered that different plants emit different sounds. A healthy plant could present a melodious frequency. An ailing one might present a sound less vibrant. Since the initial research on plant synthesizers, many resources have emerged providing devices that use Bluetooth technology to connect to the audible sound of plants. The technology converts electrical impulses of the plant and then uses biorhythmic frequencies to extract the sound. Different plants produce different sounds. It is possible to detect the health of the plant by an emitted sound. Plants can also send a visual message to its reviewer indicating how that plant is feeling.

Some plant technology resources include: Plantwave.com (which was featured by NBC news and the New York Times). Plantchoir.com is another company selling a comparative device. I am certain that plants satisfy Webster's definition of soul and consciousness.

ANIMALS AND THEIR HEALING QUALITIES

Most of us can relate to that favorite pet and the quality of life they provide for us. Some become reassuring companions. Most always they present unconditional love. They make us laugh with their unsolicited antics. They can calm anxious moments. They become an extension of our vision, provide us with an extension of mobility, become a sensory aid in detecting an impending medical issue, or be a warning system alerting us to impending danger. They can locate a lost individual, root out a smuggler, and be livestock guardians, herding assistants, or hunting retrievers.

Years earlier I worked with Wounded Warrior therapy projects. I watched a young soldier who'd lost both his legs and one arm following a Humvee explosion; launch himself atop of a 1200-pound horse to begin riding therapy. His willing partner adjusted its gait to allow the warrior to gain balance so the soldier could ride his noble steed. Horses chosen specifically for this program do not all have a calm demeanor. These noble animals seem to possess an inexplicable intuition that when caring for these special riders, and others with special needs, express incredible intelligence and caring natures.

Horses, as with most therapy ambassadors, can assess therapeutic needs and calmly provide an almost human quality to soothe emotionally and physically compromised individuals.

POWER OF WORDS

Words, sounds, and thoughts are not just inanimate expressions. They are living frequencies that carry emotional imprints that register within our energy bodies. Language is not just a compilation of phrases ... words are creation. Your words, thoughts, and actions create circuits that create frequencies that

Living Consciously

create the events and contacts in your life. The more clarity you provide through your thoughts, words and the phrases they connect with, the more beneficial synchronicities arise throughout your living world. Words can become your magic wand. The field of expression now becomes your experience.

Choose your words wisely and remember it is always better to present a positive inflection through any dialog, even when intention can be challenged. The power of thought can change outcomes, renew a planet, change the direction of a storm, generate rain, heal a body, and change the world we live in.

Thoughts become things ... choose your words and thoughts carefully.

The Alchemist Within

A new paradigm is being created in a new dimension that represents a new reality for humanity, one with awakened light codes. Humanity is leaving the 3D world behind and merging into higher evolved realms. The unfortunate side effect of this merge is chaos as the dimensions collide. At every astrologic shift of ages, as one ruling planet exits its trajectory and another emerges, there is a momentary disruption in the order of familiar life decorum. Humanity has just left the Age of Pisces and is moving into the Age of Aquarius. Each astrological age brings with it a new paradigm of God consciousness. The Age of Aquarius brings in new tendencies to embrace community values, innovation, and social equality.

When your inner awareness begins to activate you begin to notice subtle energetic sensitivities. You begin to notice a fleeting diamond light in the corner of your room. Your attention shifts to a movement you sense and turn to look at but you see nothing. You might see a mirage, a reflection usually seen as a wavering iridescent field rising up from a hot street. This distortion makes you question your sanity. All these appearances, and more, are alerting you that your spiritual team is close by and watching over you. With your new found curiosity awakened, you now begin to research those elements that will enhance your life.

There are a few essential elements to incorporate into your awareness before you can fully access your internal alchemy. The first element is to understand you are a particle of divine light. What does that mean? Your life adventure is masked to allow you to master the life goals you desired to achieve while on the Earth plane.

In actuality you reside within a universal complex of divine oneness. You are a part (particle) of the divine light of creation. You are not disconnected from the source of all creation because you are a particle of that divine source.

Humanity, as a whole, is shifting between two units of awareness: Acknowledgement of their spiritual being and the human one. These two compositions are merging to assist in your becoming one complete individual; spiritually aware, yet able to live in a physical reality without compromising who you are. This represents becoming heart centered. This is the language of God/Source . . . no matter how you refer to a sovereign energy, God is love.

You are already a master but you have come to resolve unfinished stories. New light codes are clearing old energy systems. During your life travels it is more than likely some life challenge left an emotional residue within your soul memory. This is where your awakening thought calls attention to storylines that are no longer beneficial for your enlightened awareness to carry.

The second essential element is for you to begin to remember and incorporate all soul aspects of your divine nature. Once you're able to remove the false programming embedded within your belief systems you will discover you are an ancient traveler having absorbed multiple life experiences throughout millennia.

Individually you are resolving past traumatic encounters, transmuting them into positive experiences and rewriting a new story. Each time you experience a life where trauma was encountered, more than likely a part of your soul splintered. Your current evolutionary phase is now calling back those splintered parts.

Dreams can be vehicles for us to engage with other timelines we inhabit in concurrent life dramas. Dreams also function as a way to make sense of something we experienced over the course of a day. If you can remember any portion of your dreamscapes, try to recall a particularly disturbing dream where you may have awoken in the morning remarking how fretful your night was because of a bothersome dream encounter. It may be that you were releasing a memory from your past, thus calling a fragmented part of your soul back to your present soul incarnation. I should also note here that a particularly disturbing dream will only be presented when the dreamer is ready to release the encounter. Some of our past life experiences have been exceptionally traumatic. Only when your energy frequency has evolved sufficiently will you encounter a past traumatic challenge to be cleared. You also access soul fragments when you visit lands you may have lived in or traveled to in your past. Your travels will awaken a memory prompting your subconscious to access the event.

Humanity is awakening and becoming new DNA engineers. This revelation allows us to rewrite our personal stories. This is huge. If we can heal the past we can embrace a new living template. When the old story looks for you and cannot find your name you have risen to a new alchemical resonance and are ready to claim your mastery.

You carry light coding within your DNA, coding that has remained dormant until you were ready to open a new field of resonance. Long ago, secret messages were encoded within ancient structures buried in time. Once humanity reached a certain vibration frequency, explorers would be led to discover the coding that would guide Earth's inhabitants to a new era in harmonious living.

When you start to engage your inner coherence those no longer matching your vibrating field will fade from your life. Once you recognize your accelerating frequency your outer world stops being random. The more coherent your inner geometry the more your external world rearranges. This is encoded through your ancient lineage.

The final element of incorporation is to learn to love unconditionally. This is one of the hardest tasks of all. It means you have to break through the programming designed to make you believe anything that doesn't look like you, doesn't act like you, or doesn't believe like you do is foreign. In fact, all the differences you encounter are the different faces of God . . . disguised to allow the individual to experience another element in the grand universal design.

Many individuals who have aligned with their inner alchemy have incorporated the vibration of the "violet flame." This is considered to be an evolved angelic ray (light form) of love and healing that transmutes life into balance.

Engaging your inner alchemy is inviting your personal spiritual resources to be part of your living world. No formal language is necessary, no specific dialogue needs to be learned, just a sincere desire to invite and incorporate a team of spiritual forces of love to become part of your physical experience. Your invitation can take a moment to initiate anywhere and to begin leading you to an on-going dialogue to engage with your alchemical team.

I want to remind you that your God-connection is not external from you but internal. You cannot be separate from the field of the Great Is. The need to drive to a sacred site or utilize formal language such as "Dear God" is not necessary. You can initiate contact anywhere, anytime, in any language. God's true house is in your heart. God is wherever you are, Always!

I do want it clear though that God and your spiritual team hear every prayer, wherever you choose to solicit communication, however you choose to deliver your message.

Most of the time it is not God who prevents you from achieving what you desire or need, it is your own misunderstanding of how your thoughts affect your daily life that prevents you from achieving a favorable result. Too often life conditioning causes you to deny success because you believe you are unworthy of receiving what you desire. As individuals, we are constantly sabotaging our own well-being through a constant barrage of buts, cant's, improbabilities, and maybe tomorrows. These are all remnants of intrusive thinking that contribute to keeping us from achieving a life of our dreams.

SIGNS OF REMEMBERING COHERENCE

As life travelers most of us want some reassurance that we are navigating life optimally or looking for some applause that we have completed a task to our best ability. Here are some signals that may affirm you are living in coherence with your highest frequency.

- Watch for a recurring thought, a sentence that repeats itself.
- Pay attention to a stranger who says exactly what you were thinking.
- Watch for repetition of number sequences, such as, 11, 22, 33, 44. This usually occurs as you randomly turn your attention to time. While traveling with a friend we would notice license plate numbers with the master acceleration of 222, 333, or 444.

- Pay attention to messages in dreams, especially if you continue recalling a repetitive dream.
- How often do you recall deja-vu, a memory that surfaces as if you'd already experienced the event?
- You notice colors are brighter and the air feels fresher.
- Food choices are more selective. If I ingest something that is not compatible with my body, there is swift acknowledgement of displeasure.
- I must be highly aware of my projected thoughts. Manifestations of my focus happen rapidly, the good manifestations and the ones ill-conceived.
- You may become more sensitive to Earth anomalies.
- You may be more sensitive to energy.
- You may interpret spiritual messages with greater accuracy.
- You now see life interference without judgment.
- You may awake without conscious awareness of time, day, or date.
- You have a strong desire to detach from drama.

- ➢ Are you experiencing more synchronicities?
- ➢ You expect positive outcomes.
- ➢ You possess greater insight to evolving life scenarios.
- ➢ Life seems less complicated.

How do you know when you are in alignment with your highest self? When whatever you are doing is in total flow, heart-centered, not needing to be forced. It's a time where "knowing" is without needing to know but being at peace with whatever needs to happen, understanding it is exactly right for you. When you reach this point, everything manifests effortlessly.

How to Receive Messages of Light

THE POWER OF PRAYER

What happens when collective prayers are received? Once again, the HeartMath Institute has been registering conscious thought frequencies since 1991. The date was 9/11/2001. Using the Hubble satellite, the HeartMath Institute registered emotional responses in the Earth's atmosphere in response to a deadly attack on humanity that was felt around the world. Hubble registered an incredible spike atmospherically in response to thousands of thoughts and prayers registered following the event.

The year was 2020 and a global pandemic spread throughout the world changing lifestyles, challenging humanity, and asking for global partners to unite to combat an invisible enemy. Even if you do not believe in prayer, the collective thoughts of humanity are sent forth commanding action from spiritual watchers.

When collective prayers are issued, collective resolutions can be expected. And if you look further behind an initial prayer, you will see additional miracles unfolding.

Prayer singularly is a powerful tool of compassion. Prayer collectively is a magical tool of intervention. It is said, "When two or three are gathered together in my name, I will grant their request" (Episcopal prayer book St. John Chrysostom).

Several years ago I wrote a cartoon illustrated book to demonstrate how God answers prayers.

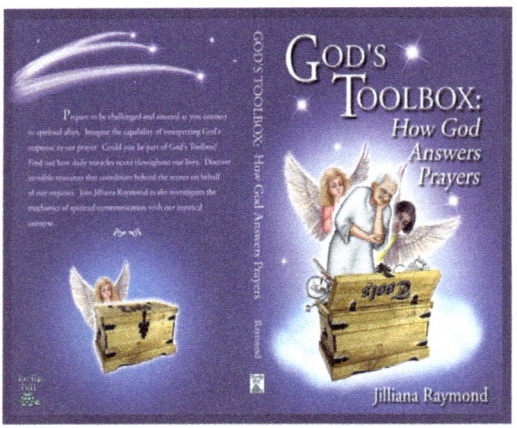

The book presents elementary ways spirit attempts to deliver answers to your inquiries. In addition to these message deliveries there are other means through which the spiritual ethers respond. Some of you have olfactory responses. This ability might allow you to smell the presence of a spirit guardian. This could be the scent of perfume if your guide is female or in my case the smell of tobacco, as my dad smoked a pipe filled with cherry tobacco. Some individuals have an ability to receive a direct audible

How to Receive Messages of Light

response (this is an internal communication that you know is not your own little voice talking back at you). You may have an inner feeling you could describe as a "knowing." What I call "spirit" will make repeated attempts to be sure you are receiving an answer to your inquiry.

If you are not listening to universal nudging you might need a more significant response. This is when you might receive what I call a "spiritual smack" from the universe. Many years ago, I received one such intervention that changed my life forever. I suspect there may be times when the universe has launched one of life's curve balls and that more than likely, if you are reading this material, you can affirm receiving one such encounter. It is that call from the ethers that literally says, "Can you hear me now?"

Messages can literally come from anywhere. Most of us are not going to see a light messenger (an angelic manifestation) materialize before us to provide an in-person response. Individually, you may also not yet be finely tuned enough to hear from an in-person delivery. However, you might hear a faint whisper that causes you to question its authenticity. I call these "spirit winks." Spirit winks can be an unexplained knock, a light that flickers, even a light that turns on or off automatically. You might just have a spontaneous thought that pops into your head. You might hear a song that continually replays in your head that has special significance. Pay attention to the lyrics. You might glance at a picture that triggers a memory of a special loved one. Perhaps dad or mom had a favorite saying that now replays in your memory that could provide you with encouragement. A spiritual hug might come as you glance at your watch and note consecutive numbers (11:11, 3:33 etc.).

When you pray or present a spiritual supplication, your prayer is intercepted by your very personal spiritual guardian network. Once a prayer request is received, it is reviewed, and your guides consult with a team of spiritual individuals who are best able to handle your request. These guides interface with your guides to arrange appropriate meetings and encounters that can best address your desire or concern. The results are forwarded to your guides and you now become connected to events, persons, or opportunities in answer to your request. Every prayer is handled in a similar fashion.

I can't emphasize enough that communication with spiritual resources is essential to complement life navigation. Spirit sees your Lights (your energy field), just as you see those little flickers of light that manifest in your room at night. When you close your eyes and begin to meditate you may see little diamonds of light.

I am going to take you on a somewhat simplified exploration on how to communicate with your spiritual guardian team. When I am counseling individuals who feel stuck because of a certain issue, I ask why not reach out to God? A general response is" I don't want to bother God for that." My immediate response is "Why not?" God is not some "Wizard of Oz" person hiding behind a curtain. God is an all-knowing, omnipresent energy. There really are no rules when establishing communication with God or any of your Light messengers. If you are truly in dire need of God's assistance, do you think you would have to go through an invocation ritual to first establish a link? Absolutely not! You would just start your conversation with, "I need help now!"

I know some of you come from traditional roots so your communication might be a little more formal such as "Dear God." You might also solicit communication with the Archangels in this manner. But your conversation might equally be as simple as: "Yo . . . God, I have been meaning to ask you about helping me find some extra cash this month." In addition, you might like to light a ritualistic candle or play soft music. If these tools make communication more meaningful for you, by all means employ these techniques. I do want it clear though that God and your spiritual team hear every prayer, wherever you choose to solicit communication, or however you choose to deliver your message. I also want you to know that God does not give more attention to one prayer over another, except in emergencies of course, where manifestation may be a bit more prompt.

Once I have established the topic(s) for my dialogue I begin to relay my agenda. I usually establish a connection by thanking God, the angels, and my spiritual guardians for being with me during the day's activities. An important annotation here is that I present my request(s) by thanking my spiritual alliance as if my prayer has already been answered. I visualize the benefit of my request as if I am already enjoying it.

When I need resolution to a specific issue I might format my prayer something like this: "Provide me with (whatever resolution I am seeking)" rather than "I would appreciate you presenting me with . . . as soon as possible." And . . . if I have reached my limit, my patience is at an all-time low, and my nerves are frazzled, my intonation gets even more intense ... something like ... "I have had it ... I expect intervention now!" In short, I make a declaration of intent, rather than a plea. I also add visual cues along with my message. The more detail I provide, the easier fulfillment will be. The spiritual ethers (or the universe, as I like to refer to them) respond very well to visual images. You might say that prayer is a package deal. If prayer is talking to God, then the quiet reflective period spent after prayer would be the meditative mode that allows you to listen for the answers.

Remembering Your Light Codes

"What is ancient within you is not a memory but a code, not a story but a blueprint."
– Lynne Kelly, *The Memory Code*

A new soul gate is now open. Solar codes are now activating dormant layers in your soul. These light codes have been buried in your DNA until your frequency was ready to be activated. This activation is bringing you memory of your soul origins. It is allowing you to at first faintly remember past life adventures. Perhaps this was a recall of an ancient land or tradition, a language familiarity, a memory how to build, a memory how to grow or a memory how to harvest. Initial symptoms of this integration might include feeling exhausted, a generalized malaise, lucid dreaming, or repetitive thoughts of creating a new direction of intrigue. Old habits, beliefs, and fragmented programs fade as your new light codes activate. Often the by-product of this activation can reveal an annoying awareness of old aches and pains. This will soon pass as your light codes continue to anchor.

Destabilizing energies have reached their tipping point. What Earth inhabitants are witnessing is a disintegration of old energy patterns. Anything no longer in balance with an intended harmonic design will not be allowed to exist.

Throughout this work you've been shown how individual choices have played a significant role in how life is experienced. You've discovered that some choices were outlined long before your entry into this physical dimension. Some predetermined choices were charted into your physical experience. These foundational dramas had to be experienced to complete unfinished stories from a previous physical journey.

With awakened light codes many previously scripted dramas can be altered. This is the gift of the light codes. It is a gift sent to humanity through universal participation and infusion of higher frequencies sent forth from our galactic neighbors. These light codes are lifting humanity into a new dimensional paradigm; one that offers the opportunity for those poised to embrace life with coherence, harmony, joy, love, wellness, and abundance.

Light codes, cloaked by outdated belief systems and years of false programming, become forgotten. This is why so much assistance from far off star systems is necessary. Galactic travelers have been summoned to help humanity to remember their ancient origins and activate dormant light codes. Star systems, much older than our own, have had years of experience to draw from. They, like us now, came from a similar Earth environment, filled with similar society dramas they learned to overcome. The best teachers are those who have direct experience in the conditions anyone would be exposed to. This is why the galactic allies can become a significant support system for our evolving world now.

By now you should realize you represent a team of individuals who are keepers of light codes. The more common reference to describe you is "light worker." As part of your life contract you accepted a special assignment from Source that you would become part of a light team that would assist in awakening humanity to remember their divine connection.

Inaudible messages or "light codes" are being broadcast from galactic sources that are activating memory patterns that will change the way you navigate through your living world and change the course of the world. Your frequency is changing the environment you live in, changing the vibration of those you associate with and calling upon all to move into a more peaceful, harmonious, and opportunistic era. You, and your fellow light team, become anchors of light on a new Earth matrix.

LANGUAGE OF SYMBOLS

The language of symbols can be seen wherever we send our awareness. Our Universe is a spiral universe. With this in mind what other mirrored objects can be identified that are spiral fields? DNA is a spiral field. Storm systems can be spiral fields. Tornados and hurricanes certainly fit this identification. Nature reflects spiral fields through her plants, through ocean dwellers that use shells, or perhaps the ancient nautilus with its coiled chambers. The spiral design can be seen in labyrinths, crops circles, mathematic equations, and reminds us to seek the unending spiral of life design as a testament to our unending journey.

Your individual guidance system may respond best to a symbolic message. What was it that the ancients knew long before any written language was created? Meditation with symbols was the architect of original thought. Messages in stone were left behind for humanity to discover at an appropriate time, placed to remind humanity of their ancient alliance and to awaken light codes buried within DNA systems.

The Egyptian civilization is the most recognizable culture that left behind symbolic pictorial language on temple walls. The ibis, the pharaoh's staff, the moon were all etched into Egyptian temple walls paying respect to Thoth. The etchings are not just images . . . they are keys. Each symbol is intended to unlock a vibrational field in your mind. The eye of Horus reminds you how to see. The activated light code vibrates through the recipient to allow the seeker to remember who they are.

There were many other civilizations that left behind their own symbolic language etched on the walls in temple sites. The ancient Greeks, the Mayans, the Aztec, and what archeologists across the globe are discovering in ancient cities are the stories of the civilizations that came before us.

Additional sacred sites around the world previously aligned with sacred geometry are coming online. Each ancient site was left to awaken humanity to their ancient heritage. These sacred sites acted as transmission towers connecting to universal frequencies designed to harmonize a civilization. Their long-dormant messages were waiting for a time when humanity could align with a new way of living and remind current inhabitants of the simplistic lifestyles of their ancient relatives.

ANIMAL MESSENGERS

Messages might come from nature. Animal messengers have delivered spiritual messages for eons. Any unusual presentation of an animal might signal a messenger. A bird might swoop down before you. You might hear the call of a hawk or screech of an owl. Several books have been written regarding the meaning of animal totems. The internet has also become a fabulous research tool.

Birds are not the only messengers. You might see a turtle crossing a street, a dolphin breaching before you, a deer running through your yard, or a fox appearing from the forest. All present messages that might align with one of your particular queries. If you've asked for an answer and are awaiting a response you might be presented with a feather or hear a melodic song outside a window.

While on an exploration to Sedona, I commissioned a native elder to escort me to the Shaman's Cave. I'd heard about the magic inside this sacred site and since it was located on a native reservation it was necessary to have a native escort. During our trek towards this sacred site several antelope were viewed bounding over the hillside. My shaman native elder remarked he'd been coming to the site for many years and had never seen the antelope. This was obviously a significant message sent to support my curious wanderings. If the presentation is unusual or infrequent, this is usually indicative of an acknowledgement or a message. Spirit knows which totem you are more likely to pay attention to and the message delivery system is always persistent.

NEW ALIGNMENT WITH INTUITIVE SENSES

Activating your light codes can be extremely easy. You've been given all the fundamental background into your origin and how simply asking for your spiritual light to be activated are the ingredients necessary to access your light codes. With your activation comes a new awareness and responsibility. You're aware that thoughts have power and create your new living world. This can be a reminder that those with awakened light codes must be more vigilant about presenting thoughts that carry a negative reflection. Manifestations become spontaneous. See if you align with some of these indicators your sensory perception may have changed.

➢ You are more sensitive to the foods you eat. What you may not have enjoyed before is now palatable.

- You're more sensitive to your environment. You may become so sensitive you become aware of impending weather anomalies.
- You may sense another's vibrational presence before they appear.
- You're aware of thoughts and the results of their projected creativity. This means you must be highly aware of your projected thinking.
- It is highly likely you will become unaware of time, day, or date. You might find it helpful to keep a calendar with you to write down important appointments.
- You may find it difficult to remember names. While I am often embarrassed that I cannot recall an individual's name, it is not a reflection on the individual, as I always enjoy being in their company.
- You have a strong desire to detach from drama.
- You find you are easily capable of dealing with conflict with assertiveness when necessary.

- You experience consistent synchronicities.

- You expect positive outcomes.

- You may wonder where an unplanned dialogue may come from. I often feel as if spirit is speaking through me.

Should your energy system become engaged in an unpleasant encounter and you're tempted to retaliate with a swift response, beware that you don't become so engulfed in the fray that you experience a swift backlash. This isn't to say you shouldn't respond to anyone who infringes on your personal boundaries. I have had individuals who strongly desire to present their personal viewpoints on subject matter I might not want to engage in. I've responded with direct language that at the time surprised me, not only with the delivery but with the fluid language presented within the dialogue.

CALLING IN ANCIENT ALLIES

I'm going to guide you through a powerful initiation. You may wish to pre-record this meditation to be able to listen to it as frequently as you desire. You may also want to read through the dialogue to be sure you are ready to assimilate the desired transformation. What I can guarantee is that when you engage your heart and soul into receiving the desired benefit, transformation will manifest rapidly. You may also download a recording from my website: www.jillianaraymond.com

Transformation begins in stillness. At first, change will be subtle, but as the energy infusion continues to anchor, it awakens ancient light codes and solicits assistance from an alliance of individuals who have traveled alongside you through many lifetimes. Their assistance in life steerage now will allow you to navigate more freely and align you with those opportunities you've been seeking.

Find a comfortable quiet space. If adding background music helps to achieve a deep inner quiet, find the appropriate music to help you relax.

Close your eyes. To achieve a deep conscious level, take three slow deep breaths, inhaling through your nose and exhaling your breath through your mouth. When any outside noise no longer distracts you, you are ready to begin.

Call in your guides to escort you to a place in your memory where you recall a particularly inviting environment. This may be emersion in a forest, a mountain retreat, a seaside vista, or an ancient land. From this space, try to observe your surroundings. Pay attention to the details within this visualization. Can you identify the era or recall the environment? Notice if there are any individuals present around you. If you are unaware of any visual details can you sense any colors or see flickering lights, those little diamonds that flash in your mind's eye? If you aren't an individual who receives visual cues, can you hear any audible messages? Can you detect any smells, perhaps the fragrance of pine boughs, the scent of the ocean, and the memory of a familiar loved one or the perfume of a familiar ally? See how many different memories you can recall . . . perhaps after you have completed your meditation journey.

With assertive authority silently say,

"I call upon those individuals of Light vibration who have traveled alongside me from all directions, from all lifetimes, to lend your energy to walk alongside me NOW. (Say with authority) RISE UP . . . AWAKEN . . . Walk With Me. Lend your energy to assist me in expanding my vibration."

"I call upon ancient light codes to ACTIVATE WITHIN ME NOW. Bring me renewed clarity, knowledge, truth, and wisdom. I CALL MY POWER BACK, so I may align with a new Earth frequency to provide me with a new experience of harmony on Earth."

"I am loving and powerful. I AM an awakened Light Being here to raise the vibration of Earth to help assist her in raising her vibration, so she may anchor her energy into her new planetary alignment within the galaxy."

"I thank my guardians. I thank those who have come to walk alongside me now to assist me in achieving my optimal life navigation. Help me expand my light that as my light expands so too will you receive the benefit from my expansion."

"And so it is."

If you continue to receive Light messages, remain in this meditative space for a while longer. When you are ready, open your eyes. Take a slow deep breath and know you have received an energy activation.

Old habits, beliefs, and fragmented programs fade as your new light codes activate. Every time you speak truth you align with your sacred geometry. Your new alignment now becomes a living code to walk into a synchronistic current. When you feel lost, disconnected, or fragmented, remember to realign with your inner truth to bring you back into alignment.

Life in Spirit

All are spiritual by design no matter what spiritual foundation provides meaning in your life; all living conscious energies arise from the spiritual realms. Many individuals will consider their life as routine and ordinary. There are no ordinary souls. You are a living legacy. Take a moment to consider how you may have inspired someone throughout your life journey.

What happens in your spiritual home is largely determined by several factors: your belief system, how you live your life, and how you are creatively designing your life in spirit. Some will return home at a pre-determined moment. Others will be called home when their work here is complete. Some are needed here to continue to anchor their light frequencies.

Spirit refers to the moment of departure as the "wind of transition." The timing of your return home has much to do with the life planning you designed while in spirit before your return to the Earth dimension. Prior to this time your spiritual team assembles to guide you home. Familiar family members, along with your spiritual guardians and a flock of angels step forward to reassure your safe return to spirit and to guide the way home. If your presence is needed to reassure a loved one still in physical residence, you will have the ability to reach out to them and stay earthbound a while longer.

TAKING THE FEAR OUT OF DYING

I have interviewed individuals who have had near death experiences. Each individual reported being immersed in an incredibly loving environment. Some of the individuals were given choices whether they would continue their physical journey while others were encouraged to return to the physical plane, all while providing them with a window into their future physical adventure. For most, the encounter provided them with sufficient support to continue living a life that mattered, and the peace of knowing what would be waiting for them upon their return. The experience also left most of these individuals profoundly changed emotionally, more at peace with an indescribable serenity about all life matters, along with a heightened awareness of spiritual presence and connectivity.

While every individual's passing is unique and experiences variable, transition brings peace and renewal to the life that has been challenged and is in decline. There are too many researchers who have documented countless depictions of afterlife interactions to ignore the seeming hallucinations of a person in transition.

Dr. Kubler-Ross, a noted American-Swiss Psychiatrist, presented the concept of the five stages of thinking of the terminally ill patient. In her documentation she acknowledged that denial, anger, bargaining, depression, and finally acceptance accompanied most individuals given that fateful prognosis. Her documentation included the emotions and experiences of over 20,000 clients. She indicates in her book *On Death and Dying,* -- "There are two certainties in life . . . that we are born into our life from spirit, and we will return there."

Noted psychologist and hypnotherapist, Dr. Michael Newton, documented client resolutions through his works, *Journey of Souls* and *Life Between Life*. And Dr. Raymond Moody, psychiatrist, physician, and author explored life after death through his case studies of near death experiences (NDE's) and patient encounters. His work is presented in his book *Life after Life*. These and other experts lend credibility to the realization that human life is much more than a singular experience. This revelation alone should bring immense comfort to any who have suffered through the loss of an important loved one and alleviate much of the concern one can experience watching the decline of a beloved individual.

Following a life-changing event, my mother (having transitioned several years earlier) floated peacefully into my bedroom wearing a green chiffon gown whispering, "Hi Honey . . . everything is going to be okay." She was beautiful, appearing as she did around the age of 30. This was nearly 35 years ago.

My dad made his physical transition in 2014. Coming to escort him home were an assortment of friends and family as he verbally acknowledged each, asking one, "Who has my Scotch?" and asking another "Where is my cane?" He was waving his hands excitedly acknowledging he hadn't seen this or that individual in a while. He had an amazing peaceful smile on his face ... not one of trauma or anguish but one of welcome home.

Since his transition he comes to remind me he is still watching over me. The lights might flicker, I might smell cherry tobacco (he liked smoking his pipe) or I might hear the faint "Hi Honey," all just to remind me I'm never alone ... and neither are you.

Too often there is a stigma that an individual needs to linger longer than necessary, either to appease an already grieving family member or carrying a belief system that there is only one life to live. Either scenario is unnecessary, as what awaits the weary physical traveler is elimination of pain and restriction, immersion into a loving environment, and preparation for a new beginning.

Several years ago I received training as a "Death Doula." I also have extensive spiritual training as a spiritual minister. As a Death Doula I could only offer solace to one individual at a time. I wanted to reach more than one individual needing hospice support to inform those ready to listen of the peaceful place they were entering and eliminate the grief and suffering that may accompany anyone going through the transition process.

I teach my clientele not to fear the process but embrace a new beginning. While death may seem permanent to many it is just the end of one life cycle. Your beloved family member may no longer reside in the physical world but they are thriving in the loving immersion of their spiritual house. Make no mistake; they will be aware of everything that is going on in your life.

WHAT MIGHT MY SPIRITUAL LIFE BE LIKE?

The question might be "What do I want to experience in my spiritual world?" Your beliefs will largely govern what you experience after your transition. However, I might be able to paint a different scenario for you to ponder. Strong beliefs shaped by religious or cultural teachings may influence how you transition into the spiritual dimensions and may influence your interaction once you've returned to your spiritual home. If you've lived life on the fringe of society or have felt your life unfairly limiting, this may influence your transition. If you harbor deep hatred, regret, guilt, or blame, take time now to resolve those feelings, so that you may be free to peacefully transition into the arms of an unconditionally loving dimension. Be assured there is no council of elders standing in judgment of any life scenario, other than your soul awaiting your own assessment of your accomplishments or regrets. There is no council of elders waiting to dole out some anticipated punishment. There is no hell, other than that which is created in your mind. There is no declared resolution for any of your interactions, other than the accountability designated by your own soul.

Eventually all will undergo a personal life review. This is like entering a 360-degree panorama reviewing everyone who has loved and offended you . . . and vice versa. You will be able to sense the emotion experienced with each encounter. For those you've loved or helped through your journey, these individuals will express a loving exchange. There is no St. Peter at the pearly gate to greet you to assign entry into the spiritual realm. For those you've compromised or who have compromised you, you will make peace without judgment and determine with whom and how you would like to rectify any unresolved conflict.

Just as you were the designer of your physical life you now design how you will experience your spiritual life. Say you want to complete some research that you began in your physical house but were unable to complete before your transition. You'll now be able to complete your research or finish your project in the abundant laboratory environments in your spiritual house. Perhaps you want to experiment with some life-sustaining discovery. You may want to create a new animal species, a new fragrance, design a new world, perhaps design a new means of transportation. You'll be able to do all this and more in the university laboratories that are available to you.

You might relish learning about ancient history and want to attend lectures or research. You can attend multiple lectures ... and if you were a speaker/teacher/expert of some particular field, you could just as easily be the teacher/speaker conducting your own lecture series. Would it surprise you to learn you can learn to play an instrument, even create one if you like, learn to paint or study from one of your favorite artists? You could design a stained glass window, create the latest fashion, attend a party (several parties), go for a walk on the beach, attend a concert, or visit with an iconic celebrity.

Perhaps you've longed to travel. This can easily be accomplished

Life in Spirit

traveling in your "light vehicle" (that's your merkabah . . . your light infused containment system).

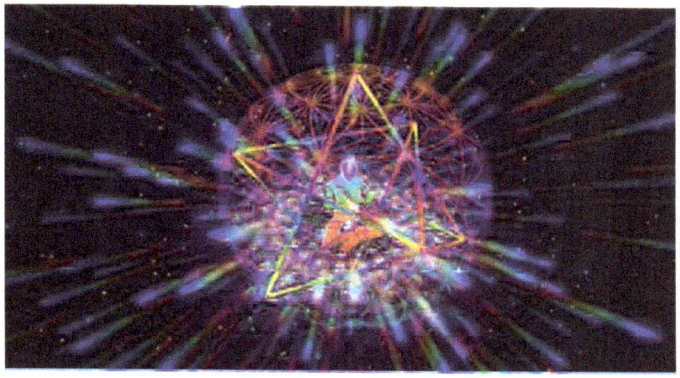

I was surprised to find this biblical reference for the merkabah: "According to verses in Ezekiel . . . the 'merkaba' consists of a chariot made of many angels being driven by the 'Likeness of a Man.'" Encyclopedia Britannica

My son's wedding. Notice the orb over my shoulder. This is a living merkabah.

Hidden Alchemy

Further investigation provides extensive ancient symbolism. The merkabah is represented in Jewish tradition as the six-pointed star. In actuality it is the convergence of a right-side-up pyramid and an upside-down pyramid that when merged represents the harmonic convergence of a man and a woman. It is also symbolic of the chariot as depicted in Tarot and referred to in the Bible as "*the chariot of fire.*" The Tarot refers to the chariot symbolism as the "*divine being who designs life's actions.*"

PREPARING BEFORE YOUR LAST BREATH

No one truly knows when that fateful moment will happen. One day you could be performing normal daily routines. The next you could be compromised by an unexpected life event. I've hosted many discussions on making final preparations before the moment of transition arrives. I discuss the importance of advising loved ones of individual final wishes, as well as informing individuals on the legacy left behind.

I've written letters to both of my sons telling them how loved they are and honoring their accomplishments. I've also made it known that I do not wish to be whisked off to a nursing home or linger in a hospital on life support. I know where I am going . . . I have no need to linger. When I transition I will be reunited with those adored individuals I left behind and we'll pick up conversation with right where we left off. When you become reunited with your loved ones you will be able to recount all the life expressions that unfolded after your departures. Spirit reunions are a blast!!

In 2019 I wrote *Before Your Last Breath* to help take the mystique and fear out of dying. I wanted loved ones coping with loss to understand the process and make it easier to handle that loss and the complications of handling an estate. When grief overcomes a living individual, it makes it far more difficult for the beloved individual to return to comfort those grieving because of the dense frequency presented by the grieving party.

To give you an idea what the departed may experience trying to comfort their loved ones . . . crossing the energy field into the physical dimension would be like crossing a muddy bog.

Some souls choose to stay close to Earth's dimensional field just to watch over living family members to help them adjust through their grief. They will of course return to surround their loved ones during any present or pending trauma.

Available on Amazon

DOCUMENTATION OF ASSETS

For those left with the arduous task of closing accounts and settling estates, a pre-planning guide can be essential. I live in a senior community where transition is an all too familiar scenario. Too often the remaining spouse or family member has no idea where to begin resolving or closing often overlooked accounts that can include those routine expenses of utilities, television, internet, phone, medical and so many more.

What if there was one place to find a glossary that included the name of the accounts, the account numbers, the contact information, thus eliminating the concern of where do I find the information I need to settle final accounting? Realizing the need to provide a source for this information, I created a workbook where anyone can list accounts and important contact info. You can download the workbook from my website at: *www.jillianaraymond.com*

In addition, having a clear set of directions for the estate executor/trix is also essential. I can't emphasize enough how important it is to provide documentation with regard to your final wishes. Prepare a will ahead of time. Those who have an estate without a will, will forfeit their estate to their specific State of Residence. As you will not be able to settle any latent family arguments over your estate once you've completed your transition, a will can be a very beneficial document designating someone to honor your final wishes.

If you do not wish extensive medical intervention you must have a DNR (Do Not Resuscitate order). This must be registered with the state and can be obtained through your physician's office or through the state. Make sure to POST your DNR notice in a very visible area, especially if emergency personnel will respond to an unexpected transition moment and the response team is not aware there is a DNR on record. You certainly would not want to be resuscitated if you are battling an irreversible diagnosis and will thus linger in a compromised state in a hospice environment that may cost your family extensive expense or drain your estate holdings drastically.

If your loved one dies at home you will want to call 911. Hopefully you've pre-arranged funeral arrangements, but the paramedics will contact the coroner or medical examiner if your loved one was not in a hospital or hospice care facility. The coroner will indicate whether an autopsy might be necessary, in which case you have no choice but to comply. If this is the scenario for your family, the coroner will provide the necessary documentation. Otherwise, your funeral director can create the death certification. This may take several weeks. Ask for at least 12 copies of the death certificates. You will need these to accompany all notifications to cancel outstanding accounts or to notify specified vendors. You will also need copies of your loved one's birth certificate and Social Security card.

More information surrounding one's transition can be acquired through internet resources, through your loved one's medical care personnel, or by reading *Before Your Last Breath*.

RESOLVING UNFINISHED ISSUES

There is no better time than the present moment to resolve unsettled issues. This may be the apology you could never make, or the thank you that you never had time to send. You may want to express that belated sympathy, or tell someone how cherished they have been in your life. Forgiveness is the key to lighten the emotional burdens absorbed during lifetimes of limitation. It is much easier to resolve issues while in the physical plane than to wait to resolve conflict from the spiritual realms. Final thoughts may be written or presented as an audible message. As you prepare to leave your current physical world, leave all the accumulated, unresolved history behind. The more coherent your inner geometry, the more your external world rearranges. And remember ... Life in spirit is a blast!

Anchoring Light Codes

At first, no significant change may be noted. Changes can be subtle at first and then, when you least expect an "aha" moment, a new awareness will be acknowledged. Several factors contribute to how or when you'll begin to experience change. Beliefs play a significant role in your evolution. If you have been exposed to years of familial, cultural, and society programming, you cannot expect to erase false programming overnight.

Not all formats work evenly for everyone. All life, however, will eventually assimilate subtle coding that will enhance everything. The amount of focus you place on accelerating spiritual evolution also factors into how quickly you ignite enhanced light coding. No need to worry, receiving light coding is guaranteed. It's just a matter of readiness.

You might question why you would want to awaken internal light codes? Living to your highest potential is essentially what your soul wants you to achieve. If there are portions of your life that do not meet your expectations, then perhaps you are limiting how you could best experience your life. Enjoying creative adventures you wish to explore with much less challenge is what is awaiting your renewed personality. Your new magnetism will attract positive synchronistic moments, new opportunities, and new contacts. The result will be a treasured life experience that others will ponder how they can achieve the happiness you project.

Awakened light coding allows you to tap into your natural intuition. Listening to personal guidance systems allows you to optimize your life experience. You will be drawn to opportunities that present you with the most advantageous experiences. By listening to your intuition you will avoid interaction with life elements that are less promising. You will know which individuals you want to align with and those you would rather avoid. It isn't that you are better than those you don't wish to interact with but that their vibration is no longer compatible with yours. You are awakening dormant signals that were long ago imprinted in your DNA. Your avoidance of individuals who you were once interactive with means you are just ahead of the awakened curve.

Awakening light codes enhances your physical system. I know way too many individuals who struggle with one health compromise or another. What if your DNA could reset to its youthful instruction to repair internal structures that may have become compromised? This is possible with new encoding. Life was meant to allow the Earth traveler a much longer tenure than our current histories would seem to support. I don't suspect any of us would rather linger in a compromised identity but if our physical structures were vibrant without compromising factors many more pleasurable life experiences could be entertained.

Exposure to a variety of sound frequencies awakens light codes within the brain. These light frequencies stimulate cellular renewal. Once light codes become activated, outdated system restrictions fade away, allowing for renewed balance to prevail. You'll no longer be drawn to elements that might not compliment your new energy system. You'll find you'll desire eating healthier. Toxic elements will automatically be eliminated. You'll have less desire to indulge in tempting decadence. You will react less to emotional intrusive triggers. Less emotional reaction equates to less stress. You're able to release emotional challenges without being drawn into a drama field.

Fear subsides as your new awareness provides an umbrella of calm, a feeling of safety surrounds you knowing you walk within an energy field of love and light. This invisible field acts as a buffer against intrusive energies. You're able to release unsavory memories of past traumas, forgiving those who became adversaries in life. You remember life is a drama played out on the Earth plane. You learn to examine all factors contributing to life experiences that may have contributed to intrusive behaviors. You learn to disassociate from individuals who no longer reflect your evolutionary frequency, wishing them well along their journey without judgment and without guilt. You become the observer of an uncomplimentary life without becoming entangled in another's life journey. You become aware that another's life experience is no longer part of your life journey.

You'll begin to ponder pathways you may have traveled. Perhaps you'll want to explore an ancient alliance. Your DNA is infused with ancient cultural traditions, memories of a past life skill or talent. Awakened light codes tune into latent abilities you find hard to explain in this life. How else can you explain emerging prodigies who possess accelerated gifts and talents?

Younger generations come onto a newer Earth with heightened talents and activated light codes. They don't need to remember where they came from, they know. Watch a child follow you in a store . . . they're drawn to your light. Their young minds have not yet been falsely programmed to forget their light coding. With activated light codes, watch how you easily navigate challenges, make decisions with authority and knowing, become a magnet to those manifestations that are in alignment with your highest potential.

You become aware of your ability to communicate with a benevolent unseen force. You understand an inaudible language that speaks directly to you providing you with guidance. You may begin to remember an ancient off-world experience, an alliance with a culture far advanced than your own awareness. Most of all, you remember a life purpose, an agreed upon assignment created long before your birth. While you long to return to a spiritual house that is filled with love, adventure, emotional freedom and renewed connection to those you've loved, you know that with activated light codes there is work to be done on Earth now with your new awareness. When your work on planet Earth is complete and you are called back to your spiritual home, you'll no longer fear going home. You know you will connect to those who have previously departed. You also know those familiar loved individuals who have since passed are aware of every life event.

As I am summarizing these messages, I am surrounded by the loving presence of my guardians supporting the messages I am delivering for those who are ready to awaken their light codes. Life was meant to be explored . . . perhaps not in the chaotic framework that seems prevalent today but to walk within the loving guidance of creation. You will begin to walk confidently through life knowing you are surrounded by the loving guidance of universal guardians and the creative source of All That Is. As an awakened Light Worker, you are the blueprint for all those who follow in your footsteps desiring to experience a new Earth that expresses life in harmony, abundance and renewed creativity.

GLOSSARY

Age of Aquarius – The Age of Aquarius is an astrological period that follows the Age of Pisces, lasting approximately 2,160 years. It is a shift in consciousness to include humanitarian and innovation concerns. Wikipedia

Akash/Akashic Record - A compilation of life events throughout time and universe stored within the soul.

Alpha Centauri - A triple star system that contains Proxima Centauri, the closest star to the Sun, about 4.2 light-years distant. The system is the third brightest star in the sky. Encyclopedia Britannica

Alpheratz – A prominent star system in the constellation of Andromeda. Alpheratz is immediately northeast of the constellation of Pegasus, it is the upper left star of the Great Square of Pegasus. Wikipedia

Andromeda – This galaxy is the closest large spiral galaxy to ours. The Andromeda galaxy is the brightest external galaxy visible in our night sky. It is the most distant galaxy humans can see with the unaided eye. Earthsky.org

Aphrodite – In Greek mythology Aphrodite was a major goddess, known for love and beauty. Her symbolic power represented bringing forth new life. This made her important to both gods and humans. https://www.greekmyths-greekmythology.com

Arcturian – Ideas regarding Arcturians are based on the readings of Dolores Cannon, an American hypnotherapist, and Edgar Cayce, an American psychic. Cayce called the Arcturians the most advanced community in the universe. Cayce saw Arcturus as a "gateway" to higher realms of consciousness. Wikipedia

Ascended Master - Ascended masters, also known as Mahatmas, are believed in several theosophical and related spiritual traditions to be spiritually enlightened beings who in past incarnations were ordinary humans. Through a series of spiritual initiations, they are said to have achieved a higher state of being. Wikipedia

Avatar – The presence of an Avatar in one's life is a call to spiritual awakening. Their teachings provide the tools to navigate the complexities of life and to ultimately understand the interconnectedness of all beings. Spiritualmojo.com

Avian – **Avian** is a metaphysical context referring to beings associated with birds, especially in spiritual beliefs surrounding Avian star seeds. They are thought to embody wisdom, freedom and communication with higher realms guiding humanity to evolution and enlightenment. Centreofexcellence.com

Candelas – An internal system of units, the base unit of luminous intensity.

Canis Major - Canis Major is home to Sirius, the brightest star in the sky. Constellation Guide

Cassiopeia – Cassiopeia is a constellation in the northern sky, named after a Greek queen in mythology. It is recognizable by its distinctive "W" shape formed by five bright stars.

Chakras – The word itself is derived from the Sanskrit word meaning "wheel." Chakras are vortexes of energy that interact with the physical and energetic bodies. Yogapedia

Christ Consciousness – The highest state of spiritual consciousness, emotional balance, wisdom. The term does not coincide with religious tradition when referring to Jesus as Christ. It is an attainment of truth and the evolution of becoming a living vessel of love. Christed - Individuals who embody the highest vibrational frequency.

Christianity – Christianity is a major religion stemming from the life, teachings, and death of Jesus of Nazareth in the 1st century CE. It has become the largest of the world's religions and, geographically, the most widely diffused. Britannica

Crystalline Earth Grid – The power source that sustains Earth frequencies.

Dead Sea Scrolls – A collection of written scrolls (containing nearly all of the Old Testament) found in a cave near the Dead Sea in the late 1940s. Wordnik

Death Doula – also called end-of life doulas or death midwives, are non-medical professionals who provide care before, during and after death.

Deja-Vu – A feeling of having previously experienced something. Wordnik

Disciple - Disciple, One who embraces and assists in spreading the teachings of another. American Heritage Dictionary

DNA – A self-replicating material that is present in nearly all living organisms as the main constituent of chromosomes. It is the carrier of genetic information.

Emerald Codes – The higher vibratory field of radiance sent from the crystal heart of Gaia. Frequencies are being sent from universal ethers to assist humanity in activation of their Divine genome. These codes are energetic imprints held both in DNA and the ascension consciousness of Gaia. The connection between these energetic imprints is raising the vibratory signature of humanity.

Essenes – The Essenes were members of a Jewish sect that flourished in Palestine from the 2nd century BCE to the 1st century CE, known for their strict communal lifestyle and dedication to Jewish law. They are often associated with the Dead Sea Scrolls, believed to be their writings. Wikipedia/Encyclopedia Britannica

Etheric – Something relating to ether, a substance thought to fill all space, often associated with spiritual realms. It can also describe a person's aura or energy field. Wikipedia

Frequency – An important parameter used in science and engineering to specify the rate of oscillatory and vibratory phenomena. Wikipedia

Gaia – Tara was an ancient name given to the Earth during the era of Lemuria and Atlantis. Gaia was the ancient name given to Earth at the time of Earth's rebirth after the sinking of Lemuria and Atlantis.

Galactic Council – The Galactic Council is a coalition representing thousands of intelligent biological species. They are a peacekeeping force first and foremost. The Galactic Council negotiates non-aggression pacts between its various member worlds.

Geomagnetic Field – A magnetic field associated with Earth. It is primarily dipolar (i.e., it has two poles, the north and south magnetic poles). The field is variable, changing continuously, and its poles migrate over time.

Giza Pyramids – The Giza pyramids are ancient monumental structures located near Cairo, Egypt. They were thought to house royal tombs during the Fourth Dynasty of the Old Kingdom. Wikipedia

God Light – God is the Creator of physical light as well as the Giver of spiritual light by which we can see the truth. Light exposes that which is hidden in darkness; it shows things as they really are. To walk in the light means to know God. Got Questions.org

God Star – The Central Sun. Golden Age/Era - The Earth is now positioned in the galaxy in the 5th dimension where life forms upon the planet will experience harmony, unity consciousness, love and all its diversity for an epic 2,000 years.

Gra*al – This spelling is from the ancient Templar translation. The current familiar spelling is "grail." The original representation of the grail was a bowl-shaped vessel often associated with the Holy Grail, a legendary object with miraculous powers in Arthurian tales. Symbolically, the Holy Grail is the womb of life. It is also a symbol of spiritual wholeness. The Free Dictionary.

Hidden Alchemy

Great Is – Term applied to the omnipresent Source of the Universe.

Great Square of Pegasus – The Great Square of Pegasus consists of four stars of nearly equal brightness: Scheat, Alpheratz, Markab and Algenib. The Great Square is an asterism within the constellation Pegasus. EarthSky

Harmonic Universe – The *Harmonic Universe Theory* (HUT) book series introduces a groundbreaking view of the cosmos, describing the universe not as random chaos, but as a finely-tuned musical structure. This series blends historical physics, cosmology, and modern scientific discoveries. Harmonicuniversetheory.com

Hathor Cow Goddess – Venusian origin. Hathor is an ancient Egyptian goddess associated, later, with Isis and, earlier, with Sekhmet but eventually was considered the primeval goddess from whom all others were derived. She is usually depicted as a woman with the head of a cow, ears of a cow, or simply in cow form. Through this association, Hathor came to be regarded as the mother of the sun god Ra. World History.org

Heart Centered – An ability to be spiritually aware, yet able to live in a physical reality without compromising who you are.

Hertz Frequency – The number of Hertz (abbreviated Hz) equals the number of cycles per second. The frequency of any phenomenon with regular periodic variations can be expressed in Hertz, but the term is used most frequently in connection with alternating currents, electromagnetic waves. Britannica

Kryon – Kryon is an angelic force working with the magnetic grid of Earth's matrix. Their emergence in the 1980s has served to provide steerage for humanity during the transitional Earth shift into the higher dimensions.

Light – An electromagnetic energy created by multiple frequencies. Various color spectrums delineate the dimensional quality of the energy. Light travels on quantum waves of energy.

Light Worker – A Lightworker is a person here on Earth for a reason. Every Lightworker usually has had a challenging life. This was part of their training to understand the polarity of darkness. Light workers have the capacity to change the world. They vibrate on high frequencies and are able to assess the energy of others with ease. They may be known for their healing skills. There work can be categorized into eight classifications:

Lux Lumen – Lux is the unit of measurement for illuminance, indicating how much light hits a surface, defined as one lumen per square meter. Lumen measures the total amount of visible light emitted by a source, regardless of the area it illuminates. Wikipedia

Lyran – Lyrans are from the Lyra constellation and are considered the precursors to the human form, biology and the soul›s multidimensional DNA, the Caucasian race's thought patterns and intentions. The Lyran's soul essence originally dwelled in another universe. Mystic Knowing

Megalithic – A very large usually rough stone used in prehistoric cultures as a monument or building block.

Merkabah – The term is derived from Hebrew meaning "chariot." It often refers to a mystical concept in early Jewish mysticism that involves visions of a divine chariot associated with God's throne, particularly as described in the Book of Ezekiel. It symbolizes the connection between the physical and spiritual realms, often represented as a geometric shape in sacred geometry. Wikipedia

Metatron – The seraphim that overseas chakras. This is the access point to your Akashic Record. (consciousreminder.com)

Nubian – Nubians are a native ethnic group living in Sudan and Southern Egypt. They have a rich history dating back to ancient African civilization, a diverse culture influenced by the Nile geography. Their roots have ancient lineages. World Atlas

Hidden Alchemy

Olmec – The Olmec are considered to be the first elaborate pre-Columbian civilization of Mesoamerica (c. 1200-400 BCE) and one that is thought to have set many of the fundamental patterns evinced by later American Indian cultures of Mexico and Central America, notably the Maya and the Aztec. Britannica

Planet Taurus – Taurus' ruling planet is Venus. Venus is the planet of love and relationship. – Britannica

Pleiades – The Pleiades are also known as the Seven Sisters, an open star cluster in the northwest of the constellation Taurus. Pleiadians are known for their work with life forms. Pleiadian dolphins are an intergalactic star being that are assisting Earth and mankind in ascension.

Sirius – Sirius is the brightest star in the night sky, located in the constellation Canis Major. It is also known as the "Dog Star." Its name comes from the Greek word "Seirios," meaning "glowing." Wikipedia

Sirrah – Sirrah, also known as Alpheratz, is the brightest star in the constellation Andromeda. It is located approximately 97 light-years from Earth. Wikipedia

Shaman – A Shaman is a practitioner who interacts with the spirit world, often through altered states of consciousness, to perform healing, divination, and other spiritual services. Wikipedia

Solfeggio – A series of tones used in sacred music that is believed in alternative medicine to have different positive effects on human health.

Soul – Soul is the immaterial aspect or essence of a living being, typically believed to be immortal and separate from the body. Wikipedia

Soul Particle Retrieval – The healing of soul fracturing from past or present traumas.

Source – New thought term to reference an omnipresent energy more familiarly known as Yahweh, God, Jehovah, Ali, Mohammad, etc. It is a term that applies to an all-knowing intelligent energy.

Star Gateway – This is the stellar gateway to Source, the connection point of the 12th chakra. The color is pure gold, the access point to receive divine energy. This gate can either be open or closed determined by the vibrational frequency expressed. This chakra holds the sum of all your experiences held in the twelfth dimension. It is your divine spark and the truest essence of who you are.

Star Seed – The term star seed refers to souls, spirits, and conscious beings that have come from an alternate world to help planet Earth in some specific way. Their deep connectedness with the spiritual plane and access to ancient knowledge can inspire positive realizations amongst human beings.

Thoth – God of Wisdom Egyptian Mythology

Universe – The cosmos in which Earth is one of the planetary system

Ur – Ur, important city of ancient southern Mesopotamia (Sumer) near the Euphrates River. It became the capital of Sumerian kings of the 1st dynasty of Ur. Some of the most important preserved monuments, including the ziggurat, belong to the 3rd dynasty. Britannica

Vega – Is the brightest star in the constellation Lyra. Webster's Dictionary

Venusian – Planetary inhabitants associated with the planet Venus. Webster's Dictionary

Wind of Transition – Spiritual phrasing describing the moment a soul leaves planet Earth. Kryon – Recalibration of Humanity – Chapter Fourteen

Credits

If you are intrigued by the potential of being a star seed "Lightworker" and resonate with the possible characteristic traits of galactic travelers, it could be interesting for you to explore further ancestral origins through these and a multitude of additional resources.

Awakeningstate.com
Bible Hub: John 3:16
Cayashobo.com – Shipibo Tribe – Plant Medicine
Consciousreminder.com
Crystalwind.ca
Emerald Codes – Billy Carson
Encyclopedia Britannica
Freepik.com
Frequencygenerator.com
Galactic exploration credits belong to NASA, NoNomad.com, The Spirit Nomad, Crystalwind.ca, and YouTube
Havingfunwithhistory.com
HeartMath Institute – Hubble experiments
Heartscenter.org – David Lewis Christopher
Hertzharmony.com
The Hidden Messages in Water – Dr. Masaru Emoto
Dr. Kubler-Ross, a noted American-Swiss Psychiatrist– *On Death and Dying*
Medicine Man – Sean Connery – Lorraine Bracco- the movie
mx.pinterest.com
NASA
Old Farmer's Almanac
Plantwave.com
Plantchoir.com
Dr. Royal Rife
Dr. David Sereda
Shutterstock
Smithsonian article, (March of 2018) – *Wisdom of Trees*

Glossary

Starseed584.artstation.com
Star Trek
Star Wars
Stouchlighting.com
Thespiritnomad.com
Peter Wohlleben (a German botanist) – *Wisdom of Trees*
Yale University School of Environment
YouTube
Webster's Dictionary
Wikipedia
Wordnik
Yogapedia

RECOMMENDED READING

Gregg Braden:
    Divine Matrix
    Lost Mode of Prayer
    Spontaneous Healing of Belief
    Wisdom Codes
    Zero Point

Lee Carroll - Kryon Books – (all of them) – especially:
    Recalibration of Humanity
    The New Human: The Evolution of Humanity
    The Journey Home
    The Great Shift
    The Human Akash
    The Human Soul Revealed

Billy Carson - *Emerald Tablets of Thoth*

Paulo Coehlo – *The Alchemist*

Mike Dooley - *Top 10 Things Dead People Want You to Know*

Dr. Masaru Emoto - *Hidden Messages in Water*

Louis Hay – *You Can Heal Your Life*

David Christopher Lewis - *The 33 Initiations*

Dr. Bruce Lipton - *Biology of Belief*

Cassian Locke – *Hidden Signs of the Universe*

Dan Millman - *The Life You Were Born to Live*

Raymond Moody – *Journey of Souls*

Carolyn Myss - *Sacred Contracts*

Michael Newton - *Many Lives, Many Masters*

Debra Silverman - *The Four Elements*

AUTHOR RESOURCES

Jilliana Raymond
Contact: jillianaraymond@gmail.com
Web: jillianaraymond.com

Trained by multiple life masters, world class energy healers, and spiritual avatars, Jilliana uses the accumulated wisdom to assist others in their life transformation.

Energy Practitioner
Trained in multiple energy therapies to include:
- Craniosacral alignment: Aligning the body's axis allowing for unrestricted energy flow within the body.

- National Board of Massage Continuing Education Instructor: In-person reflexology courses available in advanced therapeutic reflexology.

- Therapeutic reflexology (Integrated Sole Energy Therapy) Practitioner: Identifies congested energy, then through massage releases stagnant centers, allowing the body to initialize release of stagnant energies causing discomfort.

Spiritual minister: Providing spiritual life solutions to release compromising life misunderstanding. Spiritual consultations available in-person, via Zoom, through phone or internet.

Transformational and award winning author:

Before Your Last Breath
The New Covenants
New Beginnings
Life Is a Spiritual Soup
God's Toolbox: How God Answers Prayers
Titles available on Amazon.

Her life research has helped hundreds transform their lives, to experience life that without emotional baggage, and begin to thrive with awakened "Light" fields of knowledge.

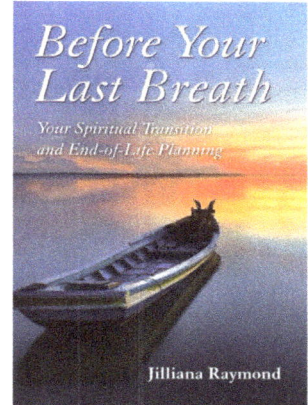
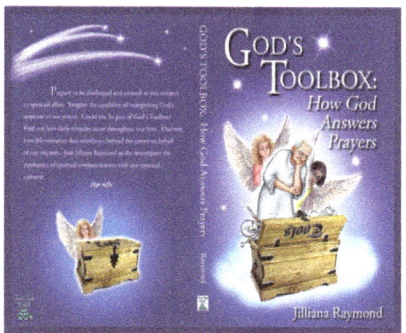

TESTIMONIALS

"Knowledgeable and informative, I would recommend Jilliana without hesitation. She is an interesting and highly qualified speaker."

Dr. Nathan Coles

"Jilliana's beautiful soul reaches out to yours, and connects you to the souls of all others, in an embrace which will "kiss the consciousness" of all souls in our wondrous Human Family. Thank you, Jilliana! "

Al Cole, from CBS Radio.
Host of the nationally syndicated talk show "People of Distinction"
Author of "*The Spirit of Romance*"

"Thanks for joining me for a wonderful interview. You deliver a beautiful message, filled with hope and inspiration! "

Jordan Rich
WBZ/CBS Radio Boston

"Your work is absolutely correct. Your words gave me chills . . . meaning = Truth! What wonderful synchronicities, as we are all working toward enlightenment of our Earth home."

Andre Ferrella, Internationally Acclaimed Visionary Artist
www.Andre.Ferrella.com

www.ingramcontent.com/pod-product-compliance
Lightning Source LLC
Chambersburg PA
CBHW061737070526
44585CB00024B/2704